Serbian Kings and Dynasties

S.T. Philips

Published by HeritageSaga Press, 2024.

While every precaution has been taken in the preparation of this book, the publisher assumes no responsibility for errors or omissions, or for damages resulting from the use of the information contained herein.

SERBIAN KINGS AND DYNASTIES

First edition. July 4, 2024.

Copyright © 2024 S.T. Philips.

ISBN: 979-8227813497

Written by S.T. Philips.

Table of Contents

Chapter 1: Introduction to Serbian Monarchy

The history of Serbian monarchy is a compelling tale of resilience, ambition, and cultural evolution. This chapter aims to provide an overarching view of the Serbian monarchy's importance, setting the stage for a deeper exploration of the individual rulers and dynasties that shaped Serbia from its early beginnings to the modern era. By examining the geographical, cultural, and historical contexts in which these monarchs ruled, we can appreciate the complexity and significance of their contributions to Serbian identity and statehood.

The Geographical and Historical Context of Serbia

Serbia, a landlocked country in Southeast Europe, is located in the central and western part of the Balkan Peninsula. Its strategic position at the crossroads of Central and Southeast Europe has historically made it a battleground for various empires and a melting pot of cultures. Bordered by Hungary to the north, Romania and Bulgaria to the east, North Macedonia to the south, and Croatia, Bosnia and Herzegovina, and Montenegro to the west, Serbia's diverse topography ranges from fertile plains in the north to mountainous regions in the south.

The early history of Serbia is intertwined with that of the broader Balkans, characterized by waves of migration and settlement. The Slavic tribes, including the Serbs, migrated to the Balkans in the 6th and 7th centuries, integrating with the indigenous Illyrian, Thracian, and Roman populations. This period laid the foundation for the formation of a distinct Serbian identity, influenced by both Western and Eastern cultures due to its geographical location.

The Importance and Role of Monarchy in Serbian History

The monarchy played a pivotal role in the formation and consolidation of the Serbian state. It served not only as a political institution but also as a unifying force that fostered national identity and cultural development. From the early medieval period to the modern era, Serbian kings and princes were instrumental in defending their territory, establishing legal and administrative systems, promoting economic growth, and fostering cultural and religious institutions.

The Serbian monarchy, like many other European monarchies, evolved through various forms of governance, from tribal chieftains and princes to fully-fledged kings and emperors. Each ruler left a unique imprint on the country's history, navigating the complex dynamics of regional and international politics, wars, alliances, and cultural exchanges.

Early Beginnings: Tribal Chieftains and the Formation of the Serbian State

Before the establishment of the first Serbian state, the region was characterized by loosely organized tribal communities. These tribes were led by chieftains who wielded considerable influence over their followers. The earliest known Serbian chieftain was Višeslav, who ruled in the early 9th century. His descendants, known as the Vlastimirović dynasty, played a crucial role in uniting the Serbian tribes and laying the foundations of the medieval Serbian state.

The Rise of the Vlastimirović Dynasty

The Vlastimirović dynasty is traditionally regarded as the first ruling dynasty of the Serbian state. The dynasty's founder, Vlastimir, ruled from 831 to 851 and is credited with consolidating Serbian territories and establishing a semblance of centralized authority. During his reign, Serbia experienced significant political and military challenges, particularly from the neighboring Byzantine Empire and the Bulgarian Khanate.

Vlastimir's reign marked the beginning of a period of relative stability and territorial expansion. His successors continued to strengthen the state, forging alliances and engaging in conflicts that shaped the geopolitical landscape of the region. The dynasty's efforts culminated in the recognition of Serbia as a distinct political entity, setting the stage for future monarchs to build upon this foundation.

The Christianization of Serbia

One of the most significant developments during the early medieval period was the Christianization of Serbia. The process of converting the Serbian population to Christianity began in the mid-9th century and was largely completed by the end of the 10th century. This transformation was facilitated by the Byzantine Empire, which sought to extend its influence over the Slavic tribes through religious and cultural assimilation.

The adoption of Christianity had profound implications for the Serbian monarchy. It not only solidified the monarch's authority by aligning it with the church but also integrated Serbia into the broader Christian world. The establishment of the Serbian Orthodox Church became a cornerstone of Serbian national identity, and subsequent monarchs played a vital role in supporting and promoting the church.

The Nemanjić Dynasty: A Golden Age

The Nemanjić dynasty, which rose to prominence in the late 12th century, is often regarded as the golden age of medieval Serbia. The dynasty's founder, Stefan Nemanja, established a powerful and centralized state that reached its zenith under the rule of his descendants. The Nemanjić kings expanded Serbian territories, fostered economic prosperity, and patronized the arts and architecture.

Stefan Nemanja's reign marked the beginning of a period of cultural and political renaissance. His son, Stefan the First-Crowned, became the first King of Serbia, officially crowned in 1217. Under the Nemanjić dynasty, Serbia achieved significant territorial expansion, extending its influence over much of the Balkans. The crowning achievement of this era was the reign of Stefan Dušan, who declared himself Emperor of the Serbs and Greeks in 1346 and codified the Serbian legal system with Dušan's Code.

The Serbian Empire and Its Decline

The Serbian Empire under Stefan Dušan represented the pinnacle of Serbian medieval statehood. Dušan's empire encompassed large parts of the Balkans, including modern-day Serbia, Montenegro, Albania, Macedonia, and northern Greece. The empire's capital, Skopje, became a vibrant cultural and political center, attracting scholars, artists, and merchants from across Europe and the Byzantine world.

However, the empire's vast expansion also sowed the seeds of its decline. The death of Stefan Dušan in 1355 led to a period of internal strife and fragmentation. His successor, Stefan Uroš V, struggled to maintain control over the diverse and far-flung territories. The weakening of central authority, combined with external pressures from the Ottoman Empire, eventually led to the disintegration of the Serbian Empire.

The Ottoman Conquest and Serbian Despotate

The fall of the Serbian Empire to the Ottomans in the late 14th century marked a significant turning point in Serbian history. Despite the loss of independence, the Serbian Despotate emerged as a semi-autonomous state under Ottoman suzerainty. The Despotate, centered in the region of Smederevo, continued to resist Ottoman encroachments while preserving Serbian culture and religious traditions.

Notable figures during this period include Despot Stefan Lazarević and Đurađ Branković, who navigated the complex political landscape of the Balkans, forging alliances with Hungary and other European powers. The resilience of the Serbian Despotate delayed the full incorporation of Serbian territories into the Ottoman Empire, allowing for the preservation of a distinct Serbian identity.

The Modern Era: From Principality to Kingdom

The 19th century witnessed the resurgence of Serbian statehood through the efforts of visionary leaders such as Milos Obrenović and Karađorđe Petrović. The First and Second Serbian Uprisings against Ottoman rule led to the establishment of the autonomous Principality of Serbia, which later evolved into the Kingdom of Serbia in 1882.

The Obrenović and Karađorđević dynasties played crucial roles in shaping modern Serbia. Milos Obrenović, as the first modern prince, implemented significant administrative and economic reforms that laid the foundation for a modern state. The Karađorđević dynasty, particularly under King Peter I, continued this trajectory, leading Serbia through the Balkan Wars and World War I.

The Kingdom of Yugoslavia and Its Challenges

The aftermath of World War I saw the creation of the Kingdom of Serbs, Croats, and Slovenes, later renamed the Kingdom of Yugoslavia. This new state aimed to unify the South Slavic peoples under a single monarchy, with King Alexander I at its helm. However, the kingdom faced numerous challenges, including ethnic tensions, political instability, and external threats.

King Alexander's assassination in 1934 and the subsequent reign of his son, Peter II, were marked by political turmoil and the looming threat of World War II. The invasion of Yugoslavia by Axis powers in 1941 led to the collapse of the monarchy and the establishment of a communist regime under Josip Broz Tito.

The Abolition of the Monarchy and the Modern Legacy

The post-war period saw the abolition of the monarchy and the establishment of the Socialist Federal Republic of Yugoslavia. The royal family went into exile, and the country embarked on a path of socialist development under Tito's leadership. Despite the monarchy's abolition, the legacy of Serbian kings continued to influence Serbian culture and national identity.

In the post-communist era, there has been a renewed interest in the Serbian monarchy, with discussions about the potential restoration of the monarchy gaining traction. The Karađorđević family, now residing in Serbia, remains a symbol of historical continuity and cultural heritage.

Conclusion: The Enduring Legacy of Serbian Kings

The history of Serbian monarchy is a testament to the resilience and adaptability of the Serbian people. From tribal chieftains to emperors, Serbian rulers navigated the complex dynamics of regional and international politics, wars, and cultural exchanges. Their contributions to state formation, cultural development, and national identity continue to resonate in contemporary Serbia.

As we delve deeper into the reigns of individual kings and dynasties in the subsequent chapters, we will uncover the rich tapestry of Serbia's royal history. Each monarch's story adds a unique thread to the fabric of Serbian heritage, offering valuable insights into the nation's past and its enduring legacy.

Chapter 2: Origins of the Serbian State

———

The early medieval period was a transformative era for the Balkans, characterized by the migration and settlement of various Slavic tribes, including the Serbs. This chapter delves into the origins of the Serbian state, tracing the development of its early political structures, cultural foundations, and key figures who laid the groundwork for the rise of the Serbian monarchy. Through this exploration, we will gain a deeper understanding of the formative years that shaped the trajectory of Serbian history.

The Arrival of the Slavs

The migration of Slavic tribes into the Balkans began in the 6th century, during a time of significant upheaval and transformation in the region. The collapse of the Western Roman Empire and the weakening of the Eastern Roman (Byzantine) Empire created a power vacuum that allowed various groups, including the Slavs, to move into the area. The Slavs, originally from the vast plains of Eastern Europe, gradually settled in the Balkans, integrating with the existing populations and establishing their own communities.

The Serbs, a South Slavic group, were among these migrating tribes. They initially settled in the areas corresponding to modern-day Serbia, Montenegro, Bosnia and Herzegovina, and parts of Croatia. The process of settlement was not instantaneous but occurred over several generations, during which the Serbs adapted to their new environment and established their presence in the region.

Early Political Structures

The early political organization of the Serbian tribes was based on a system of zupas, or territorial units, each governed by a local chieftain or zupan. These chieftains wielded significant authority within their territories, overseeing matters of governance, justice, and defense. The zupas were relatively autonomous, but they often formed alliances and confederations to address common threats and interests.

One of the earliest recorded Serbian leaders was Višeslav, who ruled in the early 9th century. Višeslav's rule marked the beginning of the Vlastimirović dynasty, which would play a crucial role in uniting the Serbian tribes and establishing a more centralized form of governance. Under Višeslav and his successors, the Serbian tribes began to consolidate their territories, laying the groundwork for the formation of a unified Serbian state.

The Vlastimirović Dynasty

The Vlastimirović dynasty is traditionally regarded as the first ruling dynasty of the Serbian state. The dynasty's founder, Vlastimir, ruled from approximately 831 to 851 and is credited with consolidating Serbian territories and establishing a semblance of centralized authority. Vlastimir's reign was marked by both military and diplomatic efforts to strengthen the nascent Serbian state.

Vlastimir's most significant military challenge came from the Bulgarian Khanate, a powerful neighboring state that sought to expand its influence over the Balkans. In the mid-9th century, the Bulgarian Khan Presian launched an invasion of Serbian territories. Vlastimir successfully repelled the invasion, securing Serbian independence and solidifying his authority. This victory not only enhanced Vlastimir's prestige but also demonstrated the growing strength and cohesion of the Serbian state.

Christianization and Cultural Transformation

The process of Christianization was a pivotal moment in the history of the Serbian state. The adoption of Christianity began in earnest during the mid-9th century, influenced by both the Byzantine Empire and the Frankish Empire. The decision to embrace Christianity had profound implications for the Serbian state, as it facilitated closer ties with powerful Christian neighbors and integrated Serbia into the broader Christian world.

The Byzantine Empire played a particularly influential role in the Christianization of Serbia. Byzantine missionaries, including Saints Cyril and Methodius, were instrumental in spreading Christianity among the Slavic peoples. The establishment of the Serbian Orthodox Church, initially under the jurisdiction of the Ecumenical Patriarchate of Constantinople, provided a unifying religious framework that bolstered the authority of the Serbian rulers.

Christianization also brought about significant cultural and intellectual transformations. The introduction of the Cyrillic script, developed by Saints Cyril and Methodius, enabled the translation of religious texts into the Slavic language, making them accessible to the Serbian population. This cultural renaissance fostered the growth of literacy, education, and the arts, laying the foundation for a vibrant and distinct Serbian culture.

The Reign of Mutimir and Internal Consolidation

Following Vlastimir's death, his son Mutimir ascended to the throne. Mutimir's reign, which lasted from approximately 851 to 891, was marked by efforts to consolidate internal control and strengthen the central authority of the Serbian state. One of Mutimir's key challenges was managing the complex dynamics of succession and maintaining unity among the Serbian nobility.

Mutimir faced internal opposition from his brothers, who sought to assert their own claims to power. To address this, Mutimir engaged in a series of conflicts with his brothers, ultimately emerging victorious and securing his position as the dominant ruler. These internal struggles, while challenging, underscored the need for a more centralized and cohesive governance structure.

Mutimir also continued the process of Christianization, building churches and promoting the spread of Christianity throughout Serbian territories. His reign saw the further integration of the Serbian state into the Christian world, fostering closer ties with the Byzantine Empire and other Christian states in the region.

The Succession of Petar Gojniković

The reign of Petar Gojniković, who ruled from approximately 892 to 917, marked a period of further consolidation and territorial expansion. Petar, a nephew of Mutimir, ascended to the throne following a series of power struggles that characterized the early years of his rule. Petar's reign was notable for his efforts to strengthen the central authority of the Serbian state and expand its influence over neighboring territories.

Petar's most significant military achievement was his successful campaign against the neighboring Duchy of Croatia. This campaign resulted in the annexation of additional territories, further enhancing the power and prestige of the Serbian state. Petar's reign also saw the continued spread of Christianity, with the construction of new churches and monasteries serving as centers of religious and cultural life.

However, Petar's reign was not without challenges. He faced opposition from both internal rivals and external threats, particularly from the Bulgarian Empire. The complex interplay of alliances and conflicts with neighboring states underscored the volatile nature of the political landscape in the Balkans during this period.

The Reign of Časlav Klonimirović

The reign of Časlav Klonimirović, who ruled from approximately 927 to 960, represents a significant period in the history of the Serbian state. Časlav's rule was characterized by efforts to reunite and expand Serbian territories, which had been fragmented and weakened by internal conflicts and external invasions.

Časlav's most notable achievement was his successful campaign to reunite the disparate Serbian principalities under a single ruler. By forging alliances and engaging in military campaigns, Časlav was able to consolidate his authority and restore the unity of the Serbian state. This period of reunification and expansion saw the growth of Serbian influence in the region, with Časlav establishing control over territories that extended into modern-day Bosnia, Montenegro, and Croatia.

Časlav's reign also witnessed the strengthening of the Serbian Orthodox Church. By supporting the construction of churches and monasteries and promoting religious education, Časlav contributed to the further Christianization of Serbian society. This period of religious and cultural growth laid the foundation for the flourishing of Serbian culture in the centuries to come.

The Impact of External Threats

Throughout the early medieval period, the Serbian state faced numerous external threats that shaped its development and influenced its political strategies. The Byzantine Empire, the Bulgarian Empire, and the Hungarian Kingdom were among the most significant external powers that sought to exert influence over Serbian territories.

The Byzantine Empire, in particular, played a complex role in Serbian history. While it was a source of religious and cultural influence, it also posed a significant political and military threat. The Byzantine strategy often involved a combination of direct military intervention and the use of diplomacy to maintain control over the Balkans. Serbian rulers had to navigate these complex relationships, balancing alliances and conflicts to secure their independence and territorial integrity.

The Bulgarian Empire, under rulers such as Simeon the Great, also posed a formidable threat. Bulgarian expansionist policies and military campaigns often brought them into conflict with the Serbian state. The shifting alliances and conflicts with Bulgaria were a constant feature of the early medieval period, influencing the strategic decisions of Serbian rulers.

The Legacy of Early Serbian Rulers

The early rulers of Serbia, from Višeslav to Časlav, played crucial roles in the formation and consolidation of the Serbian state. Their efforts to unify the Serbian tribes, establish centralized governance, and promote Christianization laid the groundwork for the future development of the Serbian monarchy. These rulers navigated a complex and often volatile political landscape, balancing internal and external challenges to secure their authority and expand their territories.

The legacy of these early rulers is evident in the enduring cultural and religious foundations they established. The spread of Christianity, the construction of churches and monasteries, and the promotion of literacy and education were significant achievements that had a lasting impact on Serbian society. These cultural and religious institutions became central to the identity and cohesion of the Serbian people, providing a sense of continuity and stability through subsequent periods of upheaval and change.

Conclusion: The Foundation of the Serbian State

The origins of the Serbian state are a testament to the resilience and determination of its early rulers. From the migration of Slavic tribes to the establishment of a unified and centralized state, the early medieval period was a formative era that set the stage for the rise of the Serbian monarchy. The efforts of leaders like Vlastimir, Mutimir, Petar Gojniković, and Časlav Klonimirović to consolidate their territories, promote Christianity, and navigate the complex political landscape of the Balkans were instrumental in shaping the trajectory of Serbian history.

As we move forward in this exploration of Serbian kings and their legacies, we will see how the foundations laid by these early rulers influenced the development of the Serbian state in subsequent centuries. Their achievements and challenges provide valuable insights into the evolution of Serbian monarchy and the enduring cultural and political heritage of Serbia.

Chapter 3: Vlastimirović Dynasty: The Founding Kings

The Vlastimirović dynasty represents the earliest period of organized statehood in Serbian history. This chapter delves into the reigns of the early Serbian kings and chieftains from the Vlastimirović dynasty, exploring their efforts to consolidate power, defend against external threats, and lay the foundation for a unified Serbian state. By examining the lives and legacies of these foundational rulers, we gain a deeper understanding of the early challenges and achievements that shaped the trajectory of the Serbian monarchy.

The Emergence of the Vlastimirović Dynasty

The Vlastimirović dynasty is traditionally considered the first ruling dynasty of the medieval Serbian state. It emerged during a period of significant political fragmentation and external pressures, particularly from the Byzantine Empire and the Bulgarian Khanate. The dynasty's founder, Vlastimir, is credited with consolidating various Serbian tribes and establishing a more centralized form of governance.

Vlastimir (r. 831–851)

Vlastimir, the eponymous founder of the dynasty, ruled from approximately 831 to 851. His reign marked the beginning of a concerted effort to unify the Serbian tribes under a single ruler. Vlastimir's primary challenge was to defend his nascent state against external threats, particularly from the expanding Bulgarian Khanate.

In the mid-9th century, the Bulgarian Khan Presian launched a military campaign against the Serbian territories. Vlastimir successfully repelled the Bulgarian invasion, securing Serbian independence and solidifying his authority. This victory not only enhanced Vlastimir's prestige but also demonstrated the growing strength and cohesion of the Serbian state. The successful defense against Bulgaria is a testament to Vlastimir's leadership and military acumen.

Vlastimir's reign also saw the beginning of the Christianization process in Serbia, influenced by both the Byzantine Empire and the neighboring Slavic states. While Vlastimir himself remained a pagan for most of his reign, his interactions with Christian states laid the groundwork for the eventual adoption of Christianity by his successors.

The Reign of Mutimir (r. 851–891)

Following Vlastimir's death, his son Mutimir ascended to the throne. Mutimir's reign, which lasted from approximately 851 to 891, was marked by efforts to consolidate internal control and strengthen the central authority of the Serbian state. One of Mutimir's key challenges was managing the complex dynamics of succession and maintaining unity among the Serbian nobility.

Mutimir faced internal opposition from his brothers, who sought to assert their own claims to power. The most significant conflict occurred between Mutimir and his brothers Strojimir and Gojnik. This internal strife culminated in a decisive battle, after which Mutimir emerged victorious and exiled his brothers to the Bulgarian court. This act of decisively dealing with internal dissent helped stabilize his rule and secure his position as the dominant ruler.

Mutimir's reign is also notable for his diplomatic engagement with the Byzantine Empire. In an effort to strengthen ties with Byzantium, Mutimir sent his sons to Constantinople, where they were baptized and educated. This act of sending hostages was a common practice to ensure loyalty and foster diplomatic relations. The baptism of his sons marked a significant step towards the Christianization of Serbia, aligning the state more closely with the Byzantine cultural and religious sphere.

Petar Gojniković (r. 892–917)

The succession of Petar Gojniković, the son of Gojnik, marked a continuation of the Vlastimirović dynasty's efforts to strengthen and expand the Serbian state. Petar's reign, from approximately 892 to 917, was characterized by military campaigns and territorial consolidation.

Petar Gojniković's most significant military achievement was his successful campaign against the neighboring Duchy of Croatia. This campaign resulted in the annexation of additional territories, further enhancing the power and prestige of the Serbian state. Petar's reign also saw the continued spread of Christianity, with the construction of new churches and monasteries serving as centers of religious and cultural life.

However, Petar's reign was not without challenges. He faced opposition from both internal rivals and external threats, particularly from the Bulgarian Empire. In 917, Petar was captured by the Bulgarians and taken to Preslav, where he later died. Despite these challenges, Petar's reign contributed to the further consolidation of the Serbian state and its territorial expansion.

Pavle Branović (r. 917–921)

Following the capture and death of Petar Gojniković, the Bulgarian Empire installed Pavle Branović, a relative of the Vlastimirović family, as the ruler of Serbia. Pavle's reign, which lasted from 917 to 921, was marked by his efforts to maintain his position amidst the complex political dynamics of the region.

Pavle's rule was challenged by Zaharija Pribislavljević, another member of the Vlastimirović dynasty. Zaharija sought to reclaim the throne with the support of the Byzantine Empire. The ensuing conflict between Pavle and Zaharija highlighted the ongoing struggle for power within the Serbian ruling family and the influence of external powers in determining the leadership of Serbia.

In 921, Pavle was overthrown by Zaharija, who succeeded in securing the throne with Byzantine support. Pavle's short reign underscores the turbulent nature of Serbian politics during this period, with frequent changes in leadership and the significant impact of foreign interventions.

Zaharija Pribislavljević (r. 921–924)

Zaharija Pribislavljević's reign, from 921 to 924, was characterized by his efforts to assert Serbian independence from both Bulgarian and Byzantine influences. His ascension to the throne was supported by the Byzantine Empire, which sought to counter Bulgarian expansion in the region.

Zaharija's reign was marked by his conflict with the Bulgarian Empire, particularly with Tsar Simeon I. In 924, Simeon launched a military campaign against Serbia, resulting in Zaharija's defeat and subsequent flight to Croatia. The Bulgarian forces ravaged Serbian territories, and the state temporarily fell under Bulgarian control.

Despite his short reign, Zaharija's efforts to assert Serbian independence and resist external domination highlight the ongoing struggle for autonomy that characterized the early history of the Serbian state. His conflict with Bulgaria also underscores the broader geopolitical dynamics of the Balkans during this period.

Časlav Klonimirović (r. 927–960)

The reign of Časlav Klonimirović represents a significant period of reunification and expansion for the Serbian state. Časlav, who ruled from approximately 927 to 960, is often regarded as one of the most important rulers of the early medieval Serbian state.

Časlav's rise to power followed a period of Bulgarian dominance over Serbian territories. After the death of Tsar Simeon in 927, Časlav returned to Serbia and successfully reunited the fragmented Serbian principalities. His efforts to consolidate his authority and restore the unity of the Serbian state were marked by both military and diplomatic initiatives.

One of Časlav's most notable achievements was his successful campaign to extend Serbian control over territories that included modern-day Bosnia, Montenegro, and parts of Croatia. This period of territorial expansion significantly enhanced the power and influence of the Serbian state in the region.

Časlav's reign also saw the strengthening of the Serbian Orthodox Church. By supporting the construction of churches and monasteries and promoting religious education, Časlav contributed to the further Christianization of Serbian society. This period of religious and cultural growth laid the foundation for the flourishing of Serbian culture in the centuries to come.

The Legacy of the Vlastimirović Dynasty

The Vlastimirović dynasty's contributions to the formation and consolidation of the Serbian state are of immense historical significance. The efforts of rulers like Vlastimir, Mutimir, Petar Gojniković, and Časlav Klonimirović to unify the Serbian tribes, defend against external threats, and promote Christianity laid the groundwork for the future development of the Serbian monarchy.

The legacy of the Vlastimirović dynasty is evident in the enduring cultural and religious foundations they established. The spread of Christianity, the construction of churches and monasteries, and the promotion of literacy and education were significant achievements that had a lasting impact on Serbian society. These cultural and religious institutions became central to the identity and cohesion of the Serbian people, providing a sense of continuity and stability through subsequent periods of upheaval and change.

The Vlastimirović dynasty's ability to navigate the complex political landscape of the Balkans, balancing internal and external challenges, set a precedent for future Serbian rulers. Their legacy is a testament to the resilience and determination of the early Serbian state, which, despite numerous challenges, succeeded in establishing a distinct and enduring national identity.

Conclusion: The Founding Kings and the Roots of Serbian Statehood

The Vlastimirović dynasty represents the foundational period of Serbian statehood. From the reign of Vlastimir to the reunification efforts of Časlav Klonimirović, the early rulers of Serbia played crucial roles in shaping the trajectory of the Serbian state. Their efforts to unify the Serbian tribes, establish centralized governance, and promote Christianity were instrumental in laying the foundations for a unified and cohesive Serbian state.

As we continue our exploration of Serbian kings and their legacies, we will see how the foundations laid by the Vlastimirović dynasty influenced the development of the Serbian state in subsequent centuries. The achievements and challenges faced by these early rulers provide valuable insights into the evolution of Serbian monarchy and the enduring cultural and political heritage of Serbia.

Chapter 4: Stefan Nemanja and the Founding of the Nemanjić Dynasty

The establishment of the Nemanjić dynasty marks a pivotal chapter in Serbian history. This chapter will explore the life and reign of Stefan Nemanja, the founder of the Nemanjić dynasty, and his efforts to consolidate power, expand territories, and promote religious and cultural development. Stefan Nemanja's legacy set the stage for a golden age in medieval Serbian history, characterized by political stability, territorial expansion, and cultural flourishing.

Early Life and Rise to Power

Stefan Nemanja was born around 1113 in Ribnica (modern-day Podgorica, Montenegro). His father, Zavida, was a nobleman and a member of the Serbian ruling family, which at the time was divided by internal conflicts and influenced by neighboring powers such as the Byzantine Empire and the Kingdom of Hungary. Nemanja's early years were shaped by these political tensions and the complex dynamics of regional power struggles.

In 1166, Nemanja emerged as a significant political figure when he became the Grand Prince of Raška, the central region of medieval Serbia. His rise to power was marked by a successful rebellion against his brothers, who had divided the Serbian territories among themselves. Nemanja's victory in this familial conflict allowed him to consolidate his authority and begin the process of unifying the Serbian lands under his rule.

Consolidation of Power

One of Nemanja's first actions as Grand Prince was to secure his position through a combination of military prowess and diplomatic maneuvering. He sought to strengthen his rule by building alliances with neighboring states and securing the loyalty of the Serbian nobility. Nemanja's marriage to Ana, a noblewoman from the Byzantine-influenced region of Duklja (modern-day Montenegro), helped solidify his political alliances and bolster his legitimacy as a ruler.

Nemanja's efforts to consolidate power also involved asserting his independence from the Byzantine Empire, which had long exerted influence over Serbian territories. In 1167, Nemanja openly rebelled against Byzantine authority, seeking to establish a more autonomous and unified Serbian state. This rebellion marked the beginning of a series of conflicts with Byzantium, as Nemanja sought to expand his territories and reduce Byzantine control.

Military Campaigns and Territorial Expansion

Stefan Nemanja's reign was characterized by a series of military campaigns aimed at expanding Serbian territories and securing his borders. One of his most significant military achievements was the conquest of the coastal region of Duklja (modern-day Montenegro) in the late 1160s. This victory not only expanded Serbia's territory but also provided Nemanja with access to the Adriatic Sea, enhancing his strategic and economic position.

Nemanja's expansionist ambitions also led him to engage in conflicts with the Kingdom of Hungary and the Byzantine Empire. In 1183, he launched a successful campaign against the Byzantine-held territories of Niš and Skopje, further expanding his domain. These military successes solidified Nemanja's reputation as a formidable leader and increased his influence in the Balkans.

In addition to his military campaigns, Nemanja also focused on fortifying his existing territories. He oversaw the construction of numerous fortresses and fortified towns, which helped secure his borders and protect his realm from external threats. These defensive measures were crucial in maintaining the stability and security of the Serbian state during his reign.

Religious and Cultural Contributions

Stefan Nemanja's reign is notable not only for his military and political achievements but also for his significant contributions to the religious and cultural development of Serbia. A devout Christian, Nemanja was deeply committed to promoting Orthodox Christianity and strengthening the Serbian Orthodox Church.

In 1190, Nemanja convened a church council at Ras, the capital of medieval Serbia, where he sought to reorganize and strengthen the church's structure. He established new dioceses and appointed loyal bishops, ensuring that the church remained closely aligned with his rule. This reorganization helped consolidate the church's influence and laid the foundation for the eventual autocephaly (independence) of the Serbian Orthodox Church.

One of Nemanja's most enduring legacies is his patronage of monasticism and the construction of numerous monasteries. The most famous of these is the Studenica Monastery, founded by Nemanja in 1190. Located in central Serbia, Studenica became a major center of religious and cultural life, renowned for its architecture, frescoes, and manuscript production. The monastery's influence extended beyond Serbia, attracting monks and scholars from across the Orthodox Christian world.

In addition to Studenica, Nemanja also founded the Hilandar Monastery on Mount Athos in Greece, in collaboration with his son, Saint Sava. Hilandar became one of the most important spiritual centers for Serbs, playing a crucial role in the development of Serbian monasticism and religious culture. These monasteries served not only as religious institutions but also as centers of learning, art, and culture, contributing to the broader cultural renaissance of medieval Serbia.

Abdication and Monastic Life

In 1196, at the height of his power, Stefan Nemanja made the remarkable decision to abdicate the throne and retire to monastic life. This decision was influenced by his deep religious convictions and his desire to spend his remaining years in spiritual contemplation. Nemanja's abdication was a carefully planned transition of power, ensuring a smooth succession and the continued stability of the Serbian state.

Nemanja was succeeded by his middle son, Stefan, who was later known as Stefan the First-Crowned. This succession was significant because Stefan was crowned by the Pope in 1217, becoming the first King of Serbia and marking the formal recognition of the Serbian state by the Western Christian world. Nemanja's abdication and the peaceful transfer of power to his son set a precedent for future successions and contributed to the stability and continuity of the Nemanjić dynasty.

After his abdication, Nemanja took the monastic name Simeon and retired to the Studenica Monastery, which he had founded. He later joined his son Sava at the Hilandar Monastery on Mount Athos. As a monk, Simeon continued to play an influential role in the religious and cultural life of Serbia. His spiritual legacy, along with his political and military achievements, cemented his status as one of the most revered figures in Serbian history.

Legacy of Stefan Nemanja

Stefan Nemanja's legacy is multifaceted, encompassing his achievements as a military leader, a political consolidator, and a religious patron. His efforts to unify the Serbian territories and establish a centralized state laid the foundation for the rise of the Nemanjić dynasty, which would oversee a golden age of Serbian medieval history.

Nemanja's military campaigns and territorial expansions significantly enhanced Serbia's power and influence in the Balkans. His successful defense against external threats and strategic conquests established Serbia as a formidable regional power. These achievements provided the stability and security necessary for the subsequent cultural and economic development of the Serbian state.

As a patron of the Serbian Orthodox Church, Nemanja played a crucial role in strengthening the church's structure and influence. His support for monasticism and the construction of monasteries fostered a cultural and religious renaissance that had a lasting impact on Serbian society. The monasteries founded by Nemanja, such as Studenica and Hilandar, became centers of spiritual and cultural life, contributing to the preservation and enrichment of Serbian heritage.

Nemanja's abdication and transition to monastic life exemplify his deep religious convictions and his commitment to ensuring a stable succession. His decision to retire as a monk reflected the symbiotic relationship between the Serbian state and the Orthodox Church, a relationship that would continue to shape Serbian identity and governance for centuries.

Conclusion: The Founding of a Dynasty

Stefan Nemanja's reign marked the beginning of a new era in Serbian history. His efforts to consolidate power, expand territories, and promote religious and cultural development set the stage for the rise of the Nemanjić dynasty, which would oversee a period of unprecedented growth and prosperity for medieval Serbia. Nemanja's legacy as a unifier, warrior, and patron of the church has left an indelible mark on Serbian history, earning him a revered place in the pantheon of great Serbian leaders.

As we continue our exploration of the Nemanjić dynasty in the subsequent chapters, we will see how Nemanja's successors built upon his foundation, leading Serbia through a golden age of political stability, territorial expansion, and cultural flourishing. The achievements and challenges faced by the Nemanjić kings provide valuable insights into the evolution of the Serbian state and the enduring legacy of Stefan Nemanja.

Chapter 5: Stefan the First-Crowned and the Golden Age

S tefan Nemanja's abdication in 1196 marked the beginning of a new era in Serbian history, as his son, Stefan the First-Crowned, ascended to the throne. Stefan the First-Crowned's reign was a significant period of political consolidation, territorial expansion, and cultural flourishing, often referred to as the Golden Age of Serbia. This chapter delves into the life and reign of Stefan the First-Crowned, his achievements, and his contributions to the development of the medieval Serbian state.

Early Life and Ascension to the Throne

Stefan the First-Crowned, also known as Stefan Nemanjić, was born around 1166 as the middle son of Stefan Nemanja and Ana. His early life was marked by the political and military activities of his father, which significantly influenced Stefan's upbringing and education. As the son of a prominent ruler, Stefan was groomed for leadership, receiving both a military and a religious education.

When Nemanja abdicated in 1196, Stefan's elder brother, Vukan, expected to inherit the throne. However, Nemanja chose Stefan as his successor, believing him to be the most capable of continuing his legacy and maintaining the stability of the Serbian state. To avoid conflict, Nemanja granted Vukan control over the region of Zeta (modern-day Montenegro), thereby ensuring a smooth transition of power.

Coronation and Recognition

One of the most significant events of Stefan's reign was his coronation as the first King of Serbia. In 1217, Stefan sought and received a royal crown from Pope Honorius III, marking a critical moment in the history of the Serbian state. This act of coronation had several profound implications:

1. **International Recognition**: The coronation signified international recognition of Serbia as a kingdom, elevating its status among European states. This recognition was crucial for Serbia's diplomatic relations and its position in regional politics.
2. **Legitimization of Rule**: By receiving the crown from the Pope, Stefan legitimized his rule both domestically and internationally. This move helped solidify his authority and reduce internal dissent.
3. **Religious Diplomacy**: The coronation highlighted the delicate balance Stefan maintained between the Roman Catholic Church and the Eastern Orthodox Church. While Serbia was predominantly Orthodox, Stefan's diplomatic engagement with the Pope demonstrated his strategic acumen in navigating religious politics.

Political Consolidation and Governance

Stefan the First-Crowned's reign was characterized by efforts to consolidate and strengthen the Serbian state. He implemented a series of administrative and legal reforms aimed at centralizing authority and enhancing governance. Some of the key aspects of his governance included:

1. **Centralization of Power**: Stefan worked to centralize political power by reducing the influence of regional nobility and bringing more territories directly under his control. This

centralization helped create a more cohesive and stable state.

2. **Legal Reforms**: He introduced new legal codes that standardized laws across his territories. These reforms improved the administration of justice and promoted a sense of unity among his subjects.

3. **Feudal System**: Stefan developed the feudal system in Serbia, granting lands to loyal nobles in exchange for military service. This system helped secure the loyalty of the nobility and provided a reliable military force for the kingdom.

Military Campaigns and Territorial Expansion

Stefan the First-Crowned continued his father's legacy of military expansion and defense of Serbian territories. His reign saw several significant military campaigns aimed at expanding and securing the kingdom's borders.

1. **Conflict with Hungary**: One of Stefan's notable military engagements was against the Kingdom of Hungary. The Hungarian king, Andrew II, sought to exert influence over Serbian territories. Stefan successfully defended his kingdom, maintaining its independence and territorial integrity.

2. **Expansion into Bosnia**: Stefan also sought to expand Serbian influence into the region of Bosnia. Through a combination of military campaigns and strategic marriages, he extended his control over parts of Bosnia, further strengthening his kingdom.

3. **Defense against Byzantine and Bulgarian Threats**: Throughout his reign, Stefan had to contend with threats from the Byzantine Empire and the Bulgarian Empire. His military acumen and diplomatic strategies ensured that Serbia remained a formidable power in the region.

Cultural and Religious Contributions

Stefan the First-Crowned's reign is often remembered for its cultural and religious achievements, which laid the foundation for a flourishing of Serbian medieval culture. His contributions in this area were multifaceted:

1. **Promotion of Orthodoxy**: Despite receiving his crown from the Pope, Stefan remained a devout Orthodox Christian. He supported the Serbian Orthodox Church and worked to strengthen its institutions. His reign saw the construction and endowment of numerous churches and monasteries, which became centers of religious and cultural life.

2. **Monastic Foundations**: Stefan continued his father's tradition of monastic patronage. He founded several significant monasteries, including the Žiča Monastery, which became the seat of the Serbian archbishopric. These monastic foundations played a crucial role in preserving and promoting Serbian culture, art, and education.

3. **Cultural Renaissance**: Under Stefan's patronage, Serbia experienced a cultural renaissance. The monasteries he founded became centers of learning and artistic production, contributing to the development of Serbian literature, music, and visual arts. The manuscript production in these monastic centers preserved and disseminated important religious and cultural texts.

Relations with the Byzantine Empire

Stefan the First-Crowned maintained a complex relationship with the Byzantine Empire, marked by both conflict and diplomacy. The Byzantine Empire, under the rule of the Komnenos and Angelos dynasties, sought to exert influence over the Balkans, including Serbia.

1. **Diplomatic Engagements**: Stefan engaged in diplomatic negotiations with the Byzantine Empire, seeking to balance Serbian independence with the realities of Byzantine power. He strategically married off his children to Byzantine nobility, strengthening ties with the empire.

2. **Military Conflicts**: Despite these diplomatic efforts, Stefan's reign also saw military conflicts with Byzantium. These conflicts were often sparked by Byzantine attempts to reassert control over Serbian territories. Stefan's ability to defend his kingdom against these incursions demonstrated his military and strategic skills.

Succession and Legacy

Stefan the First-Crowned's reign came to an end in 1228 when he abdicated in favor of his son, Stefan Radoslav. Stefan's abdication was influenced by his desire to retire to monastic life, a decision reminiscent of his father, Stefan Nemanja. Taking the monastic name Symeon, he retired to the Studenica Monastery, where he continued to influence Serbian religious and cultural life until his death in 1228.

Stefan the First-Crowned's legacy is profound and multifaceted. His reign marked the formal establishment of the Serbian kingdom and its recognition by the international community. His political and military achievements laid the foundation for the subsequent expansion and consolidation of the Serbian state.

Moreover, Stefan's cultural and religious contributions had a lasting impact on Serbian society. The monasteries he founded became enduring symbols of Serbian Orthodoxy and cultural heritage. His support for the Serbian Orthodox Church strengthened its institutions and ensured its central role in Serbian life.

Conclusion: The Golden Age of Serbia

Stefan the First-Crowned's reign represents a golden age in Serbian medieval history, characterized by political stability, territorial expansion, and cultural flourishing. His achievements in consolidating power, expanding his kingdom, and promoting religious and cultural development set the stage for a period of unprecedented growth and prosperity for Serbia.

As we continue our exploration of the Nemanjić dynasty in the subsequent chapters, we will see how Stefan's successors built upon his foundation, leading Serbia through further periods of expansion and cultural renaissance. The legacy of Stefan the First-Crowned provides valuable insights into the evolution of the Serbian state and the enduring influence of the Nemanjić dynasty on Serbian history.

Chapter 6: Stefan Radoslav and Stefan Vladislav

Stefan the First-Crowned's reign set the foundation for a flourishing Serbian kingdom, but his successors faced numerous challenges as they sought to maintain and expand upon his legacy. This chapter delves into the reigns of his sons, Stefan Radoslav and Stefan Vladislav, exploring their efforts to navigate the complex political landscape of the Balkans, internal strife, and the impact of their rule on the development of medieval Serbia.

Stefan Radoslav (r. 1228–1234)

Early Life and Ascension to the Throne

Stefan Radoslav was the eldest son of Stefan the First-Crowned and Anna Dandolo, a Byzantine princess. His upbringing was marked by his father's efforts to strengthen ties with the Byzantine Empire, as well as the religious and cultural influences of the Serbian court. Radoslav was groomed for leadership from a young age, receiving an education that emphasized both military skills and administrative knowledge.

Upon his father's abdication in 1228, Stefan Radoslav ascended to the throne. His coronation was supported by the Serbian Orthodox Church, and he took on the responsibilities of ruling a kingdom that had enjoyed relative stability and prosperity under his father. However, Radoslav's reign would soon be tested by internal and external challenges.

Byzantine Influence and Internal Strife

Radoslav's reign was significantly influenced by his connections to the Byzantine Empire through his mother. He sought to maintain these ties, hoping to secure Byzantine support for his rule. However, this reliance on Byzantine influence created tensions within the Serbian nobility, many of whom were wary of foreign intervention and sought greater autonomy.

Radoslav's efforts to assert his authority were further complicated by internal strife. His younger brothers, particularly Stefan Vladislav and Sava, posed significant challenges to his rule. Sava, who had become the first Archbishop of the autocephalous Serbian Orthodox Church, wielded considerable influence and sought to mediate the conflicts within the royal family.

In 1233, Radoslav faced a major rebellion led by his brother Vladislav, who had garnered support from dissatisfied nobles and external allies. The rebellion culminated in Radoslav's defeat and forced abdication in 1234. He fled to the Byzantine Empire, where he lived in exile for several years before eventually retiring to a monastery. His reign, though short and tumultuous, highlighted the ongoing struggles for power within the Serbian ruling family.

Stefan Vladislav (r. 1234–1243)

Rise to Power and Early Reign

Stefan Vladislav, the second son of Stefan the First-Crowned, ascended to the throne following his successful rebellion against his brother Radoslav. Vladislav's rise to power was marked by his ability to capitalize on internal discontent and secure the support of key nobles and external allies, including the Bulgarian Empire.

Vladislav's early reign focused on consolidating his authority and stabilizing the kingdom. He sought to address the grievances of the nobility and strengthen his ties with the Bulgarian Empire through marriage. Vladislav married Beloslava, the daughter of Tsar Ivan Asen II of Bulgaria, solidifying an important alliance that would play a crucial role in his reign.

Diplomatic Relations and Military Campaigns

Vladislav's reign was characterized by a combination of diplomatic efforts and military campaigns aimed at securing and expanding Serbian territories. His alliance with Bulgaria provided a strategic advantage in his conflicts with neighboring states, particularly Hungary and the remnants of the Byzantine Empire.

One of Vladislav's significant military achievements was his successful defense against Hungarian incursions into Serbian territories. The Kingdom of Hungary, seeking to expand its influence in the Balkans, posed a constant threat to Serbian sovereignty. Vladislav's military acumen and strategic alliances enabled him to repel these invasions and maintain control over key regions.

In addition to his military endeavors, Vladislav also focused on strengthening Serbia's internal governance. He continued the centralization efforts initiated by his father and worked to enhance the administrative and legal systems. His reign saw the further development of the feudal system, with lands granted to loyal nobles in exchange for military service.

Cultural and Religious Contributions

Stefan Vladislav, like his predecessors, placed significant emphasis on promoting Orthodox Christianity and supporting the Serbian Orthodox Church. His reign saw the continuation of monastic patronage and the construction of religious institutions, which played a vital role in the cultural and spiritual life of medieval Serbia.

One of Vladislav's notable contributions was the completion of the Mileševa Monastery, founded by his father. The monastery became a major center of religious and cultural activity, renowned for its frescoes and manuscript production. The frescoes of Mileševa, particularly the depiction of the "White Angel," are considered masterpieces of medieval Serbian art.

Vladislav's support for the church extended to the promotion of literacy and education. The monastic centers he patronized served as hubs of learning, where religious texts and cultural works were copied and preserved. This emphasis on education and cultural preservation helped ensure the continuity and development of Serbian cultural heritage.

Challenges and Abdication

Despite his efforts to consolidate power and promote cultural development, Vladislav's reign was not without challenges. Internal dissent continued to pose a significant threat to his rule, as rival factions within the nobility sought to assert their influence. Additionally, his reliance on Bulgarian support created tensions with other regional powers.

In 1243, Vladislav faced a significant challenge from his younger brother, Stefan Uroš I, who sought to claim the throne. Uroš garnered support from a coalition of nobles dissatisfied with Vladislav's rule. The resulting conflict culminated in Vladislav's abdication in favor of Uroš. Like his brother Radoslav, Vladislav retired to a monastery, where he spent the remainder of his life in religious contemplation.

Legacy of Stefan Radoslav and Stefan Vladislav

The reigns of Stefan Radoslav and Stefan Vladislav, though marked by internal strife and external challenges, were significant in shaping the trajectory of the Serbian kingdom during the Nemanjić dynasty. Their efforts to maintain and expand the kingdom, promote Orthodox Christianity, and support cultural development left a lasting impact on medieval Serbian society.

Stefan Radoslav's Legacy

Stefan Radoslav's short and tumultuous reign highlighted the ongoing power struggles within the Serbian royal family. His reliance on Byzantine support and the resulting tensions with the nobility underscored the challenges of balancing foreign alliances with internal stability. Despite his eventual abdication, Radoslav's reign contributed to the broader narrative of the Nemanjić dynasty's efforts to consolidate power and navigate the complex political landscape of the Balkans.

Stefan Vladislav's Legacy

Stefan Vladislav's reign was marked by significant military and diplomatic achievements, as well as notable contributions to cultural and religious life. His successful defense against external threats and efforts to stabilize the kingdom demonstrated his capability as a ruler. Vladislav's support for the Serbian Orthodox Church and his patronage of monastic institutions played a crucial role in the preservation and development of Serbian cultural heritage.

The construction and endowment of religious institutions, such as the Mileševa Monastery, left a lasting legacy that continued to influence Serbian culture for centuries. Vladislav's emphasis on education and cultural preservation helped ensure the continuity of Serbian artistic and literary traditions.

Conclusion: A Period of Transition

The reigns of Stefan Radoslav and Stefan Vladislav represent a period of transition and consolidation within the Nemanjić dynasty. Their efforts to navigate internal strife, external threats, and the complexities of regional politics were crucial in maintaining the stability and continuity of the Serbian kingdom.

As we continue our exploration of the Nemanjić dynasty in the subsequent chapters, we will see how their successors built upon their achievements and addressed the challenges they faced. The legacies of Stefan Radoslav and Stefan Vladislav provide valuable insights into the evolution of the Serbian state and the enduring influence of the Nemanjić dynasty on Serbian history. Their reigns, though marked by difficulties, contributed to the foundation upon which future rulers would build, leading Serbia through further periods of growth and prosperity.

Chapter 7: Stefan Uroš I: Expansion and Consolidation

———

Stefan Uroš I, also known as Stefan the Great, was a significant figure in the Nemanjić dynasty who ruled from 1243 to 1276. His reign marked a period of expansion and consolidation, during which he focused on strengthening the central authority, enhancing the economic prosperity of the Serbian state, and fostering cultural development. This chapter delves into Stefan Uroš I's life and reign, exploring his achievements, challenges, and contributions to the medieval Serbian state.

Early Life and Ascension to the Throne

Stefan Uroš I was born around 1223 as the third son of Stefan the First-Crowned and Anna Dandolo, a Byzantine princess. His early life was influenced by the political and cultural environment of the Serbian court, where he was groomed for leadership alongside his brothers, Radoslav and Vladislav. Uroš's upbringing included a robust education in military tactics, governance, and diplomacy, preparing him for the challenges of rulership.

Following the abdication of his brother Vladislav in 1243, Uroš ascended to the throne. His coronation was supported by a coalition of nobles who had grown dissatisfied with Vladislav's rule. Uroš's ascension marked the beginning of a new phase in Serbian history, characterized by efforts to strengthen central authority and expand territorial control.

Centralization of Power and Governance

One of Stefan Uroš I's primary goals was to centralize power and strengthen the authority of the Serbian monarchy. He sought to reduce the influence of the regional nobility and bring more territories directly under royal control. To achieve this, Uroš implemented several key strategies:

1. **Administrative Reforms**: Uroš reorganized the administrative structure of the kingdom, appointing loyal officials to key positions and establishing a more efficient system of governance. These reforms helped streamline the administration of justice, tax collection, and military conscription.
2. **Legal Reforms**: He introduced new legal codes that standardized laws across his territories, promoting fairness and reducing regional disparities. These legal reforms were instrumental in creating a more cohesive and unified state.
3. **Feudal System**: Uroš further developed the feudal system, granting lands to loyal nobles in exchange for military service and political support. This system helped secure the loyalty of the nobility and provided a reliable military force for the kingdom.

Military Campaigns and Territorial Expansion

Stefan Uroš I's reign was marked by significant military campaigns aimed at expanding Serbian territories and securing its borders. His military endeavors were characterized by both defensive and offensive strategies, ensuring the kingdom's stability and growth.

1. **Conflict with Hungary**: One of Uroš's notable military engagements was against the Kingdom of Hungary. The Hungarian kings sought to expand their influence into Serbian territories, posing a constant threat to Serbian

sovereignty. Uroš successfully defended his kingdom against Hungarian incursions, maintaining control over key regions and ensuring the kingdom's independence.

2. **Expansion into the Balkans**: Uroš also sought to expand Serbian influence into the broader Balkan region. He launched several successful campaigns against neighboring states, including Bulgaria and the remnants of the Byzantine Empire. These campaigns resulted in the annexation of additional territories, further enhancing Serbia's power and influence.

3. **Defense against the Mongols**: During Uroš's reign, the Mongol invasions posed a significant threat to Eastern Europe, including the Balkans. Uroš successfully defended his kingdom against Mongol incursions, fortifying key regions and rallying his forces to repel the invaders. His successful defense against the Mongols demonstrated his military acumen and strategic capabilities.

Economic Prosperity and Development

Stefan Uroš I was not only a skilled military leader but also an astute economic reformer. His reign saw significant efforts to enhance the economic prosperity of the Serbian state, fostering trade, agriculture, and mining.

1. **Promotion of Trade**: Uroš recognized the importance of trade for economic growth and sought to promote commercial activities within his kingdom. He established trade agreements with neighboring states and encouraged the development of trade routes. These efforts facilitated the exchange of goods and services, contributing to the overall prosperity of the kingdom.

2. **Agricultural Development**: Uroš also focused on improving

agricultural productivity, recognizing its importance for the sustenance of his population and the stability of his kingdom. He implemented agricultural reforms that promoted the use of more efficient farming techniques and the cultivation of new crops. These reforms helped increase agricultural output and ensure food security.

3. **Mining and Natural Resources**: One of the most significant economic developments during Uroš's reign was the exploitation of Serbia's rich mineral resources. He encouraged the development of mining activities, particularly in the regions of Kosovo and Rudnik, which were rich in silver and other valuable minerals. The wealth generated from mining contributed significantly to the kingdom's economy and allowed Uroš to finance his military campaigns and administrative reforms.

Cultural and Religious Contributions

Stefan Uroš I's reign was also marked by significant cultural and religious achievements. He continued the Nemanjić tradition of patronizing the Serbian Orthodox Church and promoting cultural development.

1. **Support for the Serbian Orthodox Church**: Uroš was a devout Orthodox Christian who sought to strengthen the church's influence within his kingdom. He supported the construction and endowment of numerous churches and monasteries, which became centers of religious and cultural life. These religious institutions played a crucial role in promoting Orthodox Christianity and preserving Serbian cultural heritage.

2. **Monastic Patronage**: Uroš continued the tradition of monastic patronage established by his predecessors. He

founded several significant monasteries, including the Sopoćani Monastery, known for its beautiful frescoes and architectural design. These monastic centers became hubs of artistic and intellectual activity, contributing to the cultural renaissance of medieval Serbia.

3. **Cultural Renaissance**: Under Uroš's patronage, Serbia experienced a cultural renaissance. The monasteries he supported became centers of learning and artistic production, where religious texts and cultural works were copied and preserved. This emphasis on cultural development helped ensure the continuity and enrichment of Serbian artistic and literary traditions.

Relations with Neighboring States

Stefan Uroš I's reign was characterized by complex diplomatic relations with neighboring states, including the Byzantine Empire, Hungary, and Bulgaria. His diplomatic efforts were aimed at securing alliances, maintaining peace, and expanding Serbian influence in the region.

1. **Alliance with Bulgaria**: Uroš sought to strengthen his alliance with Bulgaria through strategic marriages and diplomatic engagements. His marriage to Helen of Anjou, a noblewoman with connections to both the Byzantine and Bulgarian courts, helped solidify these ties and promote regional stability.

2. **Conflict and Diplomacy with Hungary**: While Uroš successfully defended his kingdom against Hungarian incursions, he also engaged in diplomatic efforts to maintain peace with Hungary. These efforts included negotiations and the establishment of trade agreements that benefited both kingdoms.

3. **Relations with the Byzantine Empire**: Uroš's relationship

with the Byzantine Empire was marked by both conflict and cooperation. He sought to assert Serbian independence while also engaging in diplomatic negotiations to secure Byzantine support when necessary. This delicate balance of power required careful navigation of the complex political landscape of the Balkans.

Challenges and Abdication

Despite his significant achievements, Stefan Uroš I faced several challenges during his reign. Internal dissent and power struggles within the royal family continued to pose a threat to his rule. His efforts to centralize authority and reduce the influence of the nobility were met with resistance from powerful regional lords.

In 1276, Uroš faced a significant challenge from his son, Stefan Dragutin, who sought to claim the throne. Dragutin garnered support from a coalition of nobles dissatisfied with Uroš's centralization efforts. The resulting conflict culminated in Uroš's abdication in favor of his son. Like his predecessors, Uroš retired to a monastery, where he spent the remainder of his life in religious contemplation.

Legacy of Stefan Uroš I

Stefan Uroš I's legacy is multifaceted, encompassing his achievements as a military leader, an economic reformer, and a patron of culture and religion. His reign marked a period of expansion and consolidation that significantly strengthened the Serbian state and laid the foundation for future growth and prosperity.

Military and Territorial Achievements

Uroš's successful military campaigns and territorial expansions significantly enhanced Serbia's power and influence in the Balkans. His defense against external threats, including Hungary and the Mongols, demonstrated his military acumen and strategic capabilities. These achievements provided the stability and security necessary for the kingdom's continued development.

Economic Prosperity

Uroš's economic reforms and promotion of trade, agriculture, and mining contributed to the kingdom's prosperity. His efforts to develop Serbia's natural resources, particularly its mineral wealth, provided the financial means to support his military and administrative initiatives. The economic growth during his reign laid the foundation for the kingdom's continued prosperity in the years to come.

Cultural and Religious Contributions

Uroš's support for the Serbian Orthodox Church and his patronage of cultural institutions played a crucial role in preserving and promoting Serbian cultural heritage. The monasteries and churches he founded became centers of religious and cultural life, fostering a cultural renaissance that enriched Serbian society. His emphasis on education and artistic production helped ensure the continuity and development of Serbian artistic and literary traditions.

Conclusion: A Legacy of Strength and Prosperity

Stefan Uroš I's reign represents a significant period in the history of the Serbian medieval state. His efforts to centralize power, expand territories, and promote economic and cultural development set the stage for a period of growth and prosperity that would continue under his successors. Uroš's legacy as a military leader, economic reformer, and cultural patron has left an enduring mark on Serbian history, earning him a revered place in the annals of the Nemanjić dynasty.

As we continue our exploration of the Nemanjić dynasty in the subsequent chapters, we will see how Stefan Uroš I's successors built upon his achievements and addressed the challenges they faced. The legacies of these rulers provide valuable insights into the evolution of the Serbian state and the enduring influence of the Nemanjić dynasty on Serbian history. Their reigns, though marked by both triumphs and challenges, contributed to the foundation upon which future rulers would build, leading Serbia through further periods of expansion and cultural flourishing.

Chapter 8: Stefan Dragutin and Stefan Milutin

The Nemanjić dynasty continued its influence over the Serbian kingdom through the reigns of Stefan Dragutin and Stefan Milutin. These two brothers, both sons of Stefan Uroš I, played crucial roles in navigating the complexities of internal power struggles, regional politics, and diplomatic relations. Their reigns were marked by significant territorial changes, strategic marriages, and ongoing efforts to strengthen the Serbian state.

Stefan Dragutin (r. 1276–1282)

Early Life and Ascension to the Throne

Stefan Dragutin was born around 1252 as the eldest son of Stefan Uroš I and Helen of Anjou. His early years were shaped by the political and military activities of his father, who was focused on expanding and consolidating the Serbian kingdom. Dragutin was groomed for leadership, receiving an education that emphasized both military skills and administrative knowledge.

In 1276, Dragutin rebelled against his father, Stefan Uroš I, with the support of a faction of nobles dissatisfied with Uroš's centralization efforts. Dragutin's rebellion was successful, and Uroš abdicated in his favor. Dragutin's ascension to the throne marked the beginning of a new phase in Serbian history, characterized by both internal and external challenges.

Reign and Challenges

Dragutin's reign was relatively short and fraught with difficulties. His initial efforts focused on consolidating his power and addressing the concerns of the nobility who had supported his rebellion. However, Dragutin's reign was marked by significant challenges, including conflicts with neighboring states and internal dissent.

1. **Conflict with Bulgaria and Hungary**: Dragutin faced ongoing conflicts with both Bulgaria and Hungary, two powerful neighboring states that sought to exert influence over Serbian territories. These conflicts strained Dragutin's resources and required strategic diplomacy and military efforts to maintain Serbian sovereignty.
2. **Internal Strife**: Dragutin's efforts to centralize power and reduce the influence of the nobility were met with resistance from powerful regional lords. This internal strife weakened his authority and created instability within the kingdom.

In 1282, Dragutin suffered a serious injury during a hunting accident, which significantly affected his ability to rule. As a result, he abdicated the throne in favor of his younger brother, Stefan Milutin. Despite abdicating, Dragutin retained control over a significant portion of Serbian territories, including the regions of Mačva, Usora, and Soli. These territories became known as the "Kingdom of Srem."

Stefan Milutin (r. 1282–1321)

Ascension to the Throne

Stefan Milutin, born around 1253, was the second son of Stefan Uroš I and Helen of Anjou. Following Dragutin's abdication, Milutin ascended to the throne in 1282. His reign marked a significant period of expansion, consolidation, and cultural development for the Serbian kingdom.

Milutin's ascension was supported by a coalition of nobles and his mother, Queen Helen, who played a key role in securing his position. Unlike his brother, Milutin focused on strengthening his rule through a combination of military campaigns, strategic marriages, and diplomatic efforts.

Military Campaigns and Territorial Expansion

Stefan Milutin's reign was characterized by a series of successful military campaigns aimed at expanding Serbian territories and securing its borders. His military endeavors significantly enhanced Serbia's power and influence in the Balkans.

1. **Conquest of Macedonia**: One of Milutin's most significant military achievements was the conquest of large parts of Macedonia, which had been under Byzantine control. His campaigns in Macedonia expanded Serbian influence and secured important strategic territories.
2. **Conflict with Byzantium**: Milutin engaged in several conflicts with the Byzantine Empire, seeking to assert Serbian independence and expand his territories. Despite these conflicts, Milutin also pursued diplomatic relations with Byzantium, recognizing the importance of maintaining a balance of power in the region.
3. **Defense against Bulgaria and Hungary**: Throughout his reign, Milutin successfully defended Serbian territories against Bulgarian and Hungarian incursions. His military prowess and strategic alliances ensured the kingdom's stability and growth.

Diplomatic Marriages and Alliances

Stefan Milutin's reign was marked by his strategic use of marriages to secure alliances and strengthen his position. His marriages and those of his children played a crucial role in shaping the political landscape of the Balkans.

1. **Marriage to Anna of Bulgaria**: Milutin's marriage to Anna of Bulgaria, the daughter of Tsar George Terter, helped secure an alliance with the Bulgarian Empire. This marriage strengthened Serbia's position and facilitated cooperation between the two states.

2. **Marriage to Simonida of Byzantium**: In 1299, Milutin married Simonida, the daughter of Byzantine Emperor Andronikos II Palaiologos. This marriage was a significant diplomatic achievement, solidifying an alliance with the Byzantine Empire and securing Milutin's position as a major regional power.

3. **Marriages of His Children**: Milutin also arranged strategic marriages for his children, furthering his diplomatic efforts. These marriages helped secure alliances with neighboring states and reinforced Serbia's influence in the region.

Cultural and Religious Contributions

Stefan Milutin was a devout Orthodox Christian who played a significant role in promoting the Serbian Orthodox Church and supporting cultural development. His reign saw a cultural renaissance, characterized by the construction of churches and monasteries and the patronage of the arts.

1. **Church Construction and Endowment**: Milutin founded and endowed numerous churches and monasteries throughout his kingdom. One of his most notable contributions was the construction of the Gračanica

Monastery, a masterpiece of medieval Serbian architecture and art. These religious institutions became centers of spiritual and cultural life, contributing to the preservation and enrichment of Serbian heritage.

2. **Support for Monasticism**: Milutin's patronage of monasticism played a crucial role in promoting Orthodox Christianity and fostering cultural development. Monasteries such as Hilandar on Mount Athos and Banjska Monastery in Kosovo became hubs of religious and cultural activity, attracting scholars, artists, and theologians.

3. **Cultural Renaissance**: Under Milutin's patronage, Serbia experienced a cultural renaissance. The monasteries he supported became centers of learning and artistic production, where religious texts, manuscripts, and works of art were created and preserved. This cultural flourishing enriched Serbian society and ensured the continuity of its artistic and literary traditions.

Challenges and Succession

Despite his significant achievements, Stefan Milutin's reign was not without challenges. Internal dissent and power struggles within the royal family continued to pose a threat to his rule. Milutin's efforts to centralize authority and reduce the influence of the nobility were met with resistance from powerful regional lords.

One of the most significant challenges Milutin faced was the rebellion of his son, Stefan Dečanski. In 1314, Dečanski rebelled against his father, seeking to assert his claim to the throne. The rebellion was suppressed, and Dečanski was imprisoned and later exiled to Constantinople. This conflict underscored the ongoing power struggles within the Nemanjić dynasty.

In 1321, Stefan Milutin died, leaving a complex legacy and a kingdom facing both internal and external challenges. His death marked the beginning of a new phase in Serbian history, as his son, Stefan Dečanski, sought to navigate the complexities of succession and maintain the stability of the Serbian state.

Legacy of Stefan Dragutin and Stefan Milutin

The reigns of Stefan Dragutin and Stefan Milutin were significant in shaping the trajectory of the Serbian kingdom during the Nemanjić dynasty. Their efforts to expand and consolidate the kingdom, promote Orthodox Christianity, and support cultural development left a lasting impact on medieval Serbian society.

Stefan Dragutin's Legacy

Stefan Dragutin's reign, though short and marked by challenges, was significant for its efforts to navigate the complex political landscape of the Balkans. His strategic alliances and efforts to secure regional stability contributed to the broader narrative of the Nemanjić dynasty's efforts to maintain power and influence.

Stefan Milutin's Legacy

Stefan Milutin's reign was characterized by significant military and territorial achievements, as well as notable contributions to cultural and religious life. His successful military campaigns and strategic marriages significantly enhanced Serbia's power and influence in the Balkans. Milutin's support for the Serbian Orthodox Church and his patronage of cultural institutions played a crucial role in preserving and promoting Serbian cultural heritage.

The construction and endowment of religious institutions, such as the Gračanica Monastery, left a lasting legacy that continued to influence Serbian culture for centuries. Milutin's emphasis on education, artistic production, and cultural preservation helped ensure the continuity and development of Serbian artistic and literary traditions.

Conclusion: A Period of Expansion and Cultural Flourishing

The reigns of Stefan Dragutin and Stefan Milutin represent a period of expansion, consolidation, and cultural flourishing in the history of the Serbian medieval state. Their efforts to navigate internal power struggles, engage in military campaigns, and promote cultural development set the stage for further growth and prosperity under their successors.

As we continue our exploration of the Nemanjić dynasty in the subsequent chapters, we will see how Stefan Milutin's successors built upon his achievements and addressed the challenges they faced. The legacies of these rulers provide valuable insights into the evolution of the Serbian state and the enduring influence of the Nemanjić dynasty on Serbian history. Their reigns, marked by both triumphs and challenges, contributed to the foundation upon which future rulers would build, leading Serbia through further periods of expansion and cultural flourishing.

Chapter 9: Stefan Dečanski: The Rebuilder King

Stefan Dečanski, also known as Stefan Uroš III, ruled Serbia from 1321 to 1331. His reign was marked by efforts to rebuild and stabilize the Serbian state after the turbulent period that followed his father's death. Stefan Dečanski faced numerous challenges, including internal strife, external threats, and the need for economic and cultural restoration. This chapter explores the life and reign of Stefan Dečanski, examining his achievements, struggles, and lasting contributions to medieval Serbia.

Early Life and Imprisonment

Stefan Dečanski was born around 1276, the son of Stefan Milutin and his second wife, Princess Elizabeth of Hungary. His early life was marked by the political and military endeavors of his father, who was focused on expanding and consolidating the Serbian kingdom. Dečanski received a comprehensive education that included military training and an understanding of governance.

However, his relationship with his father became strained due to succession disputes. In 1314, Dečanski rebelled against Stefan Milutin, seeking to assert his claim to the throne. The rebellion was suppressed, and Dečanski was captured and imprisoned. According to some accounts, he was blinded on the orders of his father, though modern historians debate the extent of his injuries. Dečanski was then exiled to Constantinople, where he remained until his father's death in 1321.

Ascension to the Throne

Upon the death of Stefan Milutin in 1321, a power struggle ensued within the Serbian court. Despite his previous rebellion and exile, Stefan Dečanski managed to garner the support of key nobles and was able to ascend to the throne. His main rival for the throne was his half-brother, Stefan Konstantin, who was ultimately defeated and killed in the ensuing conflict.

Stefan Dečanski's ascension marked the beginning of a period of rebuilding and consolidation. His primary goals were to stabilize the kingdom, restore economic prosperity, and strengthen the central authority weakened by internal strife and external threats during his father's later years.

Military Campaigns and Territorial Defense

Stefan Dečanski's reign was characterized by several significant military campaigns aimed at defending and expanding Serbian territories. His military endeavors were essential in maintaining the stability and security of the kingdom.

Battle of Velbazhd (1330)

One of the most significant military achievements of Stefan Dečanski's reign was the Battle of Velbazhd (modern-day Kyustendil) in 1330. This battle was fought against the Bulgarian Empire, which had become a major threat to Serbian sovereignty. The conflict was precipitated by Bulgarian Tsar Michael Shishman, who sought to expand his influence over Serbian territories.

The Serbian forces, led by Stefan Dečanski and his son Stefan Dušan, achieved a decisive victory at Velbazhd. The Bulgarian army was defeated, and Tsar Michael Shishman was killed in the battle. This victory significantly enhanced Stefan Dečanski's reputation and secured Serbian dominance in the region. The Battle of Velbazhd is considered one of the most important military engagements in medieval Serbian history, as it solidified Serbia's position as a major power in the Balkans.

Defense Against Hungarian Incursions

In addition to his conflicts with Bulgaria, Stefan Dečanski also faced threats from the Kingdom of Hungary. The Hungarian kings sought to exert influence over Serbian territories, particularly in the northern regions. Dečanski successfully defended his kingdom against Hungarian incursions, maintaining control over key territories and ensuring the kingdom's stability.

Political and Economic Reforms

Stefan Dečanski's reign was not only marked by military achievements but also by significant political and economic reforms aimed at rebuilding the Serbian state.

Centralization of Power

Dečanski continued the efforts of his predecessors to centralize power and strengthen the authority of the Serbian monarchy. He implemented administrative reforms that reduced the influence of regional nobles and brought more territories directly under royal control. These reforms helped create a more cohesive and unified state, enhancing the efficiency of governance and the administration of justice.

Economic Restoration

One of Dečanski's primary goals was to restore economic prosperity to the kingdom, which had been weakened by internal conflicts and external threats. He focused on promoting trade, agriculture, and mining, recognizing their importance for the kingdom's economic stability and growth.

1. **Promotion of Trade**: Dečanski established trade agreements with neighboring states and encouraged the development of trade routes. These efforts facilitated the exchange of goods and services, contributing to the overall prosperity of the kingdom.
2. **Agricultural Development**: He implemented agricultural reforms that promoted the use of more efficient farming techniques and the cultivation of new crops. These reforms helped increase agricultural output and ensure food security for the population.
3. **Mining and Natural Resources**: Dečanski continued to develop Serbia's rich mineral resources, particularly in the regions of Kosovo and Rudnik. The wealth generated from mining activities provided the financial means to support his military campaigns and administrative reforms.

Cultural and Religious Contributions

Stefan Dečanski was a devout Orthodox Christian who played a significant role in promoting the Serbian Orthodox Church and supporting cultural development. His reign saw a continuation of the Nemanjić tradition of monastic patronage and the construction of religious institutions.

Monastic Patronage

Dečanski founded several significant monasteries, which became centers of religious and cultural life. One of his most notable contributions was the construction of the Visoki Dečani Monastery in Kosovo, which he founded in 1327. The monastery is renowned for its architectural beauty and its extensive collection of frescoes, which are considered masterpieces of medieval Serbian art. Visoki Dečani remains one of the most important cultural and religious sites in Serbia and is a UNESCO World Heritage Site.

Support for the Serbian Orthodox Church

Dečanski's support for the Serbian Orthodox Church extended to the promotion of religious education and the preservation of religious texts. The monasteries he founded and supported became centers of learning, where scholars and theologians gathered to study and produce important religious and cultural works. This emphasis on education and cultural preservation helped ensure the continuity and development of Serbian religious and cultural traditions.

Challenges and Conflict with Stefan Dušan

Despite his significant achievements, Stefan Dečanski's reign was not without challenges. Internal dissent and power struggles within the royal family continued to pose a threat to his rule. One of the most significant challenges Dečanski faced was the rebellion of his son, Stefan Dušan.

In the early 1330s, tensions between Dečanski and Dušan escalated, culminating in an open conflict. The exact reasons for the conflict are unclear, but it is believed that Dušan sought to assert his claim to the throne, dissatisfied with his father's rule. The rebellion was supported by a faction of nobles who were dissatisfied with Dečanski's centralization efforts and sought greater autonomy.

In 1331, Stefan Dušan successfully overthrew his father, forcing Dečanski to abdicate the throne. Dečanski was imprisoned and later died under mysterious circumstances, with some accounts suggesting that he was murdered on the orders of Dušan. Despite the tragic end to his reign, Stefan Dečanski's contributions to the Serbian state and his efforts to rebuild and stabilize the kingdom left a lasting legacy.

Legacy of Stefan Dečanski

Stefan Dečanski's legacy is multifaceted, encompassing his achievements as a military leader, a political reformer, and a patron of culture and religion. His reign marked a period of rebuilding and consolidation that significantly strengthened the Serbian state and laid the foundation for future growth and prosperity.

Military and Territorial Achievements

Dečanski's successful military campaigns, particularly the Battle of Velbazhd, significantly enhanced Serbia's power and influence in the Balkans. His defense against external threats, including Bulgaria and Hungary, demonstrated his military acumen and strategic capabilities. These achievements provided the stability and security necessary for the kingdom's continued development.

Political and Economic Reforms

Dečanski's political and economic reforms helped centralize power and restore economic prosperity to the kingdom. His efforts to promote trade, agriculture, and mining contributed to the overall growth and stability of the Serbian state. These reforms laid the foundation for the kingdom's continued prosperity in the years to come.

Cultural and Religious Contributions

Dečanski's support for the Serbian Orthodox Church and his patronage of cultural institutions played a crucial role in preserving and promoting Serbian cultural heritage. The monasteries and churches he founded became centers of religious and cultural life, fostering a cultural renaissance that enriched Serbian society. His emphasis on education and artistic production helped ensure the continuity and development of Serbian artistic and literary traditions.

Conclusion: The Rebuilder King

Stefan Dečanski's reign represents a significant period in the history of the Serbian medieval state. His efforts to rebuild and stabilize the kingdom, expand territories, and promote economic and cultural development set the stage for further growth and prosperity under his successors. Dečanski's legacy as a military leader, political reformer, and cultural patron has left an enduring mark on Serbian history, earning him a revered place in the annals of the Nemanjić dynasty.

As we continue our exploration of the Nemanjić dynasty in the subsequent chapters, we will see how Stefan Dečanski's successors built upon his achievements and addressed the challenges they faced. The legacies of these rulers provide valuable insights into the evolution of the Serbian state and the enduring influence of the Nemanjić dynasty on Serbian history. Their reigns, though marked by both triumphs and challenges, contributed to the foundation upon which future rulers would build, leading Serbia through further periods of expansion and cultural flourishing.

Chapter 10: Stefan Dušan and the Serbian Empire

Stefan Dušan, also known as Dušan the Mighty, was one of the most significant rulers in Serbian history. His reign, from 1331 to 1355, marked the zenith of Serbian medieval power, characterized by territorial expansion, legal reform, and cultural flourishing. This chapter delves into the life and reign of Stefan Dušan, exploring his achievements, challenges, and the lasting impact of his legacy on the Serbian Empire.

Early Life and Ascension to the Throne

Stefan Dušan was born around 1308 as the son of Stefan Dečanski and Theodora Smilets of Bulgaria. From a young age, Dušan was exposed to the intricacies of court politics and military strategy. His father, Stefan Dečanski, ascended to the Serbian throne in 1321, and Dušan quickly became involved in the administration and defense of the kingdom.

By the early 1330s, tensions between Dušan and his father had escalated. Dissatisfied with his father's rule and seeking to assert his claim to the throne, Dušan led a rebellion against Stefan Dečanski. In 1331, Dušan successfully overthrew his father, who was imprisoned and later died under mysterious circumstances. With his father deposed, Dušan was crowned King of Serbia.

Territorial Expansion and the Creation of the Serbian Empire

Stefan Dušan's reign was marked by an ambitious campaign of territorial expansion, transforming Serbia into a powerful empire that dominated the Balkans.

Conquests and Expansion

Dušan's military campaigns were highly successful, significantly expanding Serbian territories at the expense of the Byzantine Empire and other neighboring states. Some of his notable conquests include:

1. **Thessaly and Epirus**: Dušan launched campaigns in the southern Balkans, capturing key territories such as Thessaly and Epirus. These conquests extended Serbian influence into central Greece and increased the empire's strategic and economic power.
2. **Macedonia**: One of Dušan's most significant military achievements was the conquest of large parts of Macedonia, including the important cities of Skopje and Ohrid. These territories were crucial for controlling the trade routes and consolidating Serbian power in the region.
3. **Albania and the Adriatic Coast**: Dušan also focused on expanding Serbian control over Albania and the Adriatic coast. His campaigns in these regions secured important ports and trade routes, enhancing the empire's economic prosperity and maritime influence.

The Coronation as Emperor

In 1346, Stefan Dušan took a bold step to elevate his status and legitimize his conquests. He proclaimed himself Emperor (Tsar) of the Serbs and Greeks, a title that reflected his ambition to establish a Serbian-led empire in the Balkans. This coronation took place in Skopje, where Dušan was crowned by the newly established Serbian Patriarch, Joanikije II. The proclamation of the Serbian Empire marked a significant moment in medieval Balkan history, symbolizing the peak of Serbian political and military power.

Legal and Administrative Reforms

Stefan Dušan's reign is also notable for his comprehensive legal and administrative reforms, which sought to centralize authority and standardize governance across the diverse territories of his empire.

Dušan's Code (Zakonik)

One of Dušan's most enduring legacies is the codification of Serbian law, known as Dušan's Code (Zakonik). Promulgated in 1349 and expanded in 1354, this legal code was a comprehensive collection of laws and regulations that aimed to create a uniform legal framework for the empire. Dušan's Code covered various aspects of governance, including criminal law, property rights, commerce, and the organization of the church and state.

Key features of Dušan's Code include:

1. **Centralization of Authority**: The code emphasized the central authority of the emperor and sought to reduce the power of regional nobles and feudal lords. It established strict penalties for rebellion and insubordination, reinforcing the emperor's control over his vast territories.
2. **Protection of Property Rights**: Dušan's Code included detailed provisions on property rights, inheritance, and land

tenure. These laws aimed to protect the rights of landowners and ensure the orderly transfer of property, contributing to economic stability and growth.

3. **Commerce and Trade**: The code regulated commercial activities, including trade practices, taxation, and market regulations. By promoting fair trade and reducing corruption, Dušan sought to enhance economic prosperity and encourage commerce within his empire.

4. **Religious and Moral Conduct**: Dušan's Code also addressed issues of religious and moral conduct, reflecting the close relationship between the state and the Serbian Orthodox Church. It included provisions on church organization, clergy responsibilities, and the protection of religious sites and property.

Cultural and Religious Contributions

Stefan Dušan was a devout Orthodox Christian who played a significant role in promoting the Serbian Orthodox Church and fostering cultural development. His reign saw a cultural renaissance, characterized by the construction of churches and monasteries and the patronage of the arts.

Patronage of the Serbian Orthodox Church

Dušan's support for the Serbian Orthodox Church was evident in his efforts to elevate its status and influence. In 1346, alongside his own coronation as emperor, Dušan elevated the Serbian archbishopric to the rank of a patriarchate, with Joanikije II becoming the first Serbian Patriarch. This move was significant for several reasons:

1. **Religious Independence**: The establishment of the Serbian Patriarchate symbolized the religious independence of the Serbian Church from the Byzantine Patriarchate of

Constantinople. It reinforced the idea of a Serbian-led empire with its own religious and political authority.

2. **Strengthening Orthodoxy**: Dušan's patronage of the church included the construction and endowment of numerous monasteries and churches. These religious institutions became centers of spiritual and cultural life, contributing to the preservation and promotion of Orthodox Christianity.

Monastic Patronage and Cultural Renaissance

Under Dušan's patronage, Serbia experienced a cultural renaissance. The monasteries and churches he supported became hubs of artistic and intellectual activity, attracting scholars, artists, and theologians. Notable contributions include:

1. **Church Construction**: Dušan commissioned the construction of several significant churches and monasteries, such as the Monastery of Saint Archangels near Prizren. These religious sites were renowned for their architectural beauty and intricate frescoes, reflecting the high level of artistic achievement during his reign.

2. **Manuscript Production**: The monasteries supported by Dušan became centers of manuscript production, where religious texts, legal documents, and literary works were copied and preserved. This emphasis on education and cultural preservation helped ensure the continuity and enrichment of Serbian literary and artistic traditions.

Diplomatic Relations and Regional Politics

Stefan Dušan's reign was characterized by complex diplomatic relations with neighboring states, including the Byzantine Empire, Bulgaria, Hungary, and the rising Ottoman Empire. His diplomatic efforts were aimed at securing alliances, maintaining peace, and expanding Serbian influence in the region.

Relations with the Byzantine Empire

Dušan's relationship with the Byzantine Empire was marked by both conflict and cooperation. While he sought to assert Serbian dominance over Byzantine territories, he also recognized the importance of maintaining a balance of power in the region.

1. **Military Conflicts**: Dušan's military campaigns often brought him into direct conflict with the Byzantine Empire. His conquests of Byzantine territories, including Macedonia and Epirus, significantly weakened Byzantine control in the Balkans.
2. **Diplomatic Engagements**: Despite these conflicts, Dušan engaged in diplomatic negotiations with the Byzantine emperors, seeking to secure alliances and manage regional stability. His marriage to Helena of Bulgaria, who had Byzantine connections, further strengthened his diplomatic position.

Relations with Bulgaria and Hungary

Dušan's diplomatic efforts extended to Bulgaria and Hungary, two major powers in the Balkans. His strategies included:

1. **Alliances through Marriage**: Dušan secured alliances with Bulgaria through strategic marriages. His marriage to Helena of Bulgaria and the marriages of his children to Bulgarian and Hungarian nobles helped solidify these alliances.

2. **Defense and Cooperation**: Dušan successfully defended Serbian territories against Bulgarian and Hungarian incursions, maintaining regional stability. His diplomatic engagements with these states included negotiations and the establishment of trade agreements that benefited all parties.

Challenges and the Decline of the Empire

Despite his significant achievements, Stefan Dušan's reign was not without challenges. The vastness of his empire and the diversity of its territories created difficulties in maintaining centralized control and ensuring effective governance.

Internal Strife and Rebellion

The centralization efforts outlined in Dušan's Code were met with resistance from regional nobles and feudal lords who sought greater autonomy. These internal challenges included:

1. **Noble Rebellions**: Several noble families rebelled against Dušan's centralization efforts, seeking to assert their independence and retain their traditional privileges. These rebellions were often supported by external powers, further complicating Dušan's efforts to maintain control.
2. **Regional Fragmentation**: The vast and diverse nature of Dušan's empire made it difficult to enforce uniform governance and maintain centralized authority. Regional fragmentation and local power struggles weakened the cohesion of the empire.

The Rise of the Ottoman Empire

Towards the end of Dušan's reign, the Ottoman Empire began to emerge as a significant threat to the Balkans. The Ottomans' rapid expansion posed a challenge to Dušan's efforts to maintain regional stability and protect his territories.

Death and Succession

Stefan Dušan died suddenly in 1355, leaving behind a vast and powerful empire. His death marked the beginning of a period of instability and decline for the Serbian Empire. Dušan was succeeded by his son, Stefan Uroš V, who faced significant challenges in maintaining the cohesion and stability of the empire.

Legacy of Stefan Dušan

Stefan Dušan's legacy is profound and multifaceted, encompassing his achievements as a military leader, legal reformer, and cultural patron. His reign marked the zenith of Serbian medieval power and left a lasting impact on the region.

Military and Territorial Achievements

Dušan's successful military campaigns and territorial expansions significantly enhanced Serbia's power and influence in the Balkans. His conquests extended Serbian control over large parts of the region, transforming Serbia into a dominant empire.

Legal and Administrative Reforms

Dušan's Code is one of his most enduring legacies. The comprehensive legal and administrative reforms he implemented helped centralize authority, promote economic stability, and create a uniform legal framework for the empire. These reforms laid the foundation for the continued development of the Serbian state.

Cultural and Religious Contributions

Dušan's patronage of the Serbian Orthodox Church and his support for cultural development played a crucial role in preserving and promoting Serbian cultural heritage. The monasteries and churches he founded became centers of spiritual and cultural life, fostering a cultural renaissance that enriched Serbian society.

Conclusion: The Mighty Emperor

Stefan Dušan's reign represents a pinnacle of Serbian medieval history, characterized by territorial expansion, legal reform, and cultural flourishing. His efforts to create a powerful and cohesive empire set the stage for a period of unprecedented growth and prosperity for Serbia. Dušan's legacy as a mighty emperor, legal reformer, and cultural patron has left an indelible mark on Serbian history, earning him a revered place in the annals of the Nemanjić dynasty.

As we continue our exploration of the Nemanjić dynasty in the subsequent chapters, we will see how Stefan Dušan's successors built upon his achievements and addressed the challenges they faced. The legacies of these rulers provide valuable insights into the evolution of the Serbian state and the enduring influence of the Nemanjić dynasty on Serbian history. Their reigns, marked by both triumphs and challenges, contributed to the foundation upon which future rulers would build, leading Serbia through further periods of expansion and cultural flourishing.

Chapter 11: Stefan Uroš V: The Weak King and the Decline of the Serbian Empire

———

Stefan Uroš V, known as Stefan Uroš the Weak, ruled Serbia from 1355 to 1371. His reign marked the decline of the Serbian Empire, a period characterized by internal strife, loss of centralized power, and external threats. Despite inheriting a vast and powerful empire from his father, Stefan Dušan, Uroš struggled to maintain control and cohesion over his territories. This chapter explores the life and reign of Stefan Uroš V, examining the challenges he faced, his efforts to govern, and the ultimate decline of the Serbian Empire under his rule.

Early Life and Ascension to the Throne

Stefan Uroš V was born around 1336, the only son of Stefan Dušan and his wife, Helena of Bulgaria. From a young age, Uroš was groomed for leadership, receiving an education that emphasized both military skills and administrative knowledge. However, his early years were overshadowed by his father's ambitious campaigns and efforts to consolidate the Serbian Empire.

In 1355, following the sudden death of Stefan Dušan, Stefan Uroš V ascended to the throne. At the time of his ascension, Uroš was still relatively young and inexperienced, which posed significant challenges to his ability to effectively govern a vast and diverse empire. His father's death left a power vacuum that various regional lords and external enemies sought to exploit.

Internal Strife and Loss of Centralized Power

One of the primary challenges Stefan Uroš V faced during his reign was the internal strife that plagued the Serbian Empire. The centralization efforts initiated by his father were met with resistance from powerful regional nobles who sought greater autonomy and independence.

Noble Rebellions

The most significant threat to Uroš's rule came from the regional nobility, who were dissatisfied with the centralization policies of Stefan Dušan and sought to assert their independence. Key figures in these noble rebellions included:

1. **Vukašin Mrnjavčević**: Vukašin, a powerful noble from the region of Macedonia, declared himself king and effectively ruled over large portions of the southern territories of the empire. His rebellion significantly weakened Uroš's authority and control.
2. **Lazar Hrebeljanović**: Lazar, another influential noble, established a semi-independent state in the central regions of Serbia. Although he maintained nominal loyalty to Uroš, Lazar's actions further fragmented the empire.
3. **Nikola Altomanović**: Nikola, a regional lord in western Serbia, also sought to assert his independence. His ambitions and conflicts with other nobles contributed to the overall instability of the empire.

These noble rebellions fractured the empire into semi-independent regions, each ruled by powerful lords who operated with little regard for the central authority. This fragmentation made it difficult for Uroš to effectively govern and respond to external threats.

External Threats and Military Challenges

In addition to internal strife, Stefan Uroš V's reign was marked by significant external threats, particularly from the expanding Ottoman Empire and neighboring states.

The Rise of the Ottoman Empire

The most formidable external threat to the Serbian Empire during Uroš's reign was the rapid expansion of the Ottoman Empire. The Ottomans, under the leadership of Sultan Murad I, launched a series of campaigns in the Balkans, capturing key territories and weakening the regional powers.

1. **Battle of Maritsa (1371)**: One of the most significant military engagements during Uroš's reign was the Battle of Maritsa, fought in 1371. The Serbian forces, led by Vukašin Mrnjavčević and his brother Jovan Uglješa, faced the Ottomans in a decisive battle near the Maritsa River. The Ottomans achieved a crushing victory, killing both Vukašin and Jovan and further destabilizing the Serbian Empire.
2. **Ottoman Encroachments**: The Ottomans continued to encroach on Serbian territories, capturing key regions and imposing their authority. The inability of Uroš to effectively coordinate a unified defense against the Ottoman threat contributed to the gradual erosion of Serbian power.

Conflicts with Neighboring States

Stefan Uroš V also faced conflicts with neighboring states, including Hungary, Bulgaria, and Bosnia. These conflicts further strained the resources and stability of the Serbian Empire.

1. **Hungarian Incursions**: The Kingdom of Hungary sought to expand its influence in the Balkans, launching incursions into Serbian territories. These conflicts diverted Uroš's attention

and resources, making it difficult to address the internal strife and external threats simultaneously.

2. **Bulgarian Rivalry**: The Bulgarian Empire, under Tsar Ivan Alexander, also posed a threat to Serbian territories. The rivalry between Serbia and Bulgaria weakened both states, making them more vulnerable to Ottoman expansion.

3. **Bosnian Relations**: Relations with the Bosnian Kingdom were complex and marked by both cooperation and conflict. The Bosnian Ban, Tvrtko I, sought to assert his influence over Serbian territories, further complicating Uroš's efforts to maintain control.

Efforts to Govern and Maintain Stability

Despite the numerous challenges he faced, Stefan Uroš V made efforts to govern and maintain stability within his fragmented empire. His reign saw several attempts to address internal strife, promote economic prosperity, and strengthen the Serbian Orthodox Church.

Administrative Reforms

Uroš implemented administrative reforms aimed at improving governance and reducing corruption. These reforms included:

1. **Strengthening Central Authority**: Uroš sought to reassert central authority by appointing loyal officials to key positions and reducing the power of regional nobles. However, these efforts were often undermined by the entrenched power of the nobility.

2. **Legal Reforms**: Building on his father's legal code, Uroš introduced additional legal reforms to standardize governance and promote justice. These reforms aimed to create a more cohesive legal framework for the empire, although their implementation was limited by the fragmented nature of the

state.

Economic Policies

Uroš also focused on promoting economic prosperity to support his military and administrative efforts. His economic policies included:

1. **Promotion of Trade**: Uroš encouraged trade within his territories and with neighboring states. He sought to establish trade agreements and reduce barriers to commerce, recognizing the importance of economic stability for the overall prosperity of the empire.
2. **Agricultural Development**: Efforts to improve agricultural productivity included promoting efficient farming techniques and supporting the cultivation of new crops. These initiatives aimed to increase agricultural output and ensure food security for the population.

Support for the Serbian Orthodox Church

As a devout Orthodox Christian, Uroš supported the Serbian Orthodox Church and its cultural and religious initiatives. His efforts included:

1. **Monastic Patronage**: Uroš continued the tradition of monastic patronage established by his predecessors. He supported the construction and endowment of monasteries and churches, which became centers of spiritual and cultural life.
2. **Religious Education**: Uroš promoted religious education and the preservation of religious texts. The monasteries he supported became hubs of learning, where scholars and theologians gathered to study and produce important religious and cultural works.

The Decline of the Serbian Empire

Despite his efforts to govern and maintain stability, Stefan Uroš V was ultimately unable to reverse the decline of the Serbian Empire. The combination of internal strife, external threats, and the loss of centralized power led to the fragmentation and weakening of the empire.

The Fragmentation of the Empire

By the end of Uroš's reign, the Serbian Empire had fragmented into several semi-independent regions, each ruled by powerful lords. The lack of centralized authority and the ongoing conflicts between these regional rulers further weakened the state's cohesion.

The Rise of Regional Powers

As the central authority weakened, regional powers such as Lazar Hrebeljanović and Tvrtko I of Bosnia emerged as significant players in the Balkans. These leaders sought to assert their independence and establish their own states, contributing to the overall decline of the Serbian Empire.

The Ottoman Threat

The continued expansion of the Ottoman Empire posed an existential threat to the remaining Serbian territories. The Ottomans' military prowess and strategic acumen made them a formidable adversary, and the fragmented Serbian state was ill-equipped to mount a unified defense.

Death and Succession

Stefan Uroš V died in 1371, marking the end of the Nemanjić dynasty. His death left a power vacuum that further destabilized the region. With no direct heirs, the remaining Serbian territories fell into a period of uncertainty and further fragmentation.

Legacy of Stefan Uroš V

Stefan Uroš V's legacy is complex and multifaceted. While his reign is often characterized by the decline and fragmentation of the Serbian Empire, it is important to recognize the challenges he faced and the efforts he made to govern and maintain stability.

Military and Territorial Challenges

Uroš's inability to effectively respond to internal strife and external threats significantly weakened the Serbian state. The fragmentation of the empire and the rise of regional powers were major factors in the overall decline.

Administrative and Economic Efforts

Despite the challenges, Uroš made notable efforts to implement administrative and economic reforms. His attempts to strengthen central authority, promote trade, and improve agricultural productivity reflected his commitment to stabilizing the empire.

Cultural and Religious Contributions

Uroš's support for the Serbian Orthodox Church and his patronage of cultural and religious institutions played a crucial role in preserving Serbian cultural heritage. The monasteries and churches he supported continued to be centers of spiritual and cultural life, contributing to the continuity of Serbian traditions.

Conclusion: The End of an Era

Stefan Uroš V's reign marked the end of the Nemanjić dynasty and the decline of the Serbian Empire. His struggles to maintain control over a fragmented and weakened state highlight the complexities and challenges of medieval Balkan politics. While his reign is often viewed through the lens of decline, it is important to recognize his efforts to address the myriad challenges he faced.

As we continue our exploration of Serbian history, we will examine the subsequent period of fragmentation and the rise of regional powers that sought to navigate the new political landscape of the Balkans. The legacies of these rulers, their triumphs and challenges, provide valuable insights into the evolution of the Serbian state and the enduring influence of the Nemanjić dynasty on Serbian history.

Chapter 12: The Serbian Despotate and the Struggle for Survival

———

With the death of Stefan Uroš V in 1371, the once powerful and expansive Serbian Empire disintegrated into smaller, fragmented states. The void left by the fall of the Nemanjić dynasty led to the emergence of the Serbian Despotate, a semi-independent principality that faced numerous challenges from external threats and internal strife. This chapter explores the establishment of the Serbian Despotate, the reigns of its rulers, and the struggle for survival in the face of the advancing Ottoman Empire and other regional powers.

The Formation of the Serbian Despotate

After the death of Stefan Uroš V, Serbia was left without a clear successor. The power vacuum led to the rise of regional lords who sought to establish their own dominions. Among these leaders, Prince Lazar Hrebeljanović emerged as a central figure. Lazar, who ruled from his stronghold in Kruševac, was one of the most powerful nobles in Serbia and sought to unify the fragmented territories.

Lazar Hrebeljanović (r. 1371–1389)

Prince Lazar, born around 1329, was a descendant of the Nemanjić dynasty through his mother. He married Milica, a member of the powerful Branković family, which strengthened his political position. Lazar's rule was marked by efforts to consolidate his authority and resist external threats, particularly from the Ottoman Empire.

Battle of Kosovo (1389)

One of the most significant events during Lazar's reign was the Battle of Kosovo, fought on June 28, 1389. The battle took place on the Kosovo Polje (Field of Blackbirds) and pitted the Serbian forces, led by Lazar, against the advancing Ottoman army under Sultan Murad I.

The Battle of Kosovo holds a symbolic place in Serbian history and culture. Although the battle was tactically inconclusive, both sides suffered heavy losses, and Prince Lazar was captured and executed. The battle marked a turning point, as it weakened Serbian resistance and paved the way for further Ottoman advances into the Balkans.

Despite the loss, the Battle of Kosovo became a symbol of Serbian heroism and sacrifice. Lazar's legacy was immortalized in Serbian epic poetry and folklore, portraying him as a martyr who fought bravely to defend his people and faith.

Stefan Lazarević (r. 1389–1427)

After the death of Prince Lazar, his son Stefan Lazarević inherited the title of despot and became the ruler of the Serbian Despotate. Stefan, born in 1377, was a highly educated and capable leader who sought to rebuild and stabilize the Serbian state.

Military Achievements and Diplomacy

Stefan Lazarević was a skilled military commander and diplomat. He navigated the complex political landscape of the Balkans, balancing alliances with the Ottoman Empire, Hungary, and other regional powers to ensure the survival of his despotate.

1. **Battle of Ankara (1402)**: Stefan Lazarević participated in the Battle of Ankara, where the Ottoman forces under Sultan Bayezid I were defeated by Timur (Tamerlane). Stefan's support for Bayezid earned him the title of despot from the

Byzantine Emperor Manuel II Palaiologos. The victory at Ankara temporarily halted Ottoman expansion, providing a brief respite for the Serbian Despotate.

2. **Alliance with Hungary**: Recognizing the importance of strong alliances, Stefan Lazarević forged a close relationship with the Kingdom of Hungary. He served as a loyal vassal to King Sigismund of Hungary and participated in various military campaigns. This alliance provided military and political support, helping to safeguard Serbian territories.

Cultural and Economic Flourishing

Stefan Lazarević's reign was marked by a cultural and economic renaissance. He was a patron of the arts and literature, and his court in Belgrade became a center of cultural and intellectual activity.

1. **Belgrade as the Capital**: In 1403, Stefan moved the capital of the Serbian Despotate to Belgrade. Under his rule, Belgrade was fortified and transformed into a vibrant cultural and economic hub. The city's strategic location on the confluence of the Sava and Danube rivers made it an important trade center.

2. **Literary Contributions**: Stefan Lazarević himself was an accomplished writer and poet. He authored the "Slovo ljubve" ("Word of Love"), a renowned piece of medieval Serbian literature. His court attracted scholars, artists, and theologians, contributing to the cultural enrichment of the despotate.

3. **Monastic Patronage**: Continuing the tradition of his predecessors, Stefan Lazarević supported the construction and endowment of monasteries and churches. Notable examples include the Manasija Monastery, known for its impressive architecture and frescoes. These religious

institutions played a crucial role in preserving Serbian cultural heritage.

Đurađ Branković (r. 1427–1456)

Following Stefan Lazarević's death in 1427, his nephew Đurađ Branković succeeded him as the despot of Serbia. Đurađ's reign was marked by ongoing conflicts with the Ottoman Empire and efforts to maintain the independence of the Serbian Despotate.

Military Struggles and Diplomatic Efforts

Đurađ Branković faced significant military challenges from the advancing Ottoman forces. Despite these threats, he managed to secure temporary periods of peace through diplomatic efforts and alliances.

1. **Siege of Belgrade (1440)**: One of the most notable military events during Đurađ's reign was the Siege of Belgrade in 1440. The Ottoman Sultan Murad II laid siege to the city, but Đurađ's forces, with support from Hungarian and other Christian allies, successfully defended Belgrade. The city's resilience became a symbol of Christian resistance against Ottoman expansion.

2. **Diplomatic Maneuvering**: Đurađ Branković skillfully navigated the complex political landscape of the time, balancing alliances with Hungary, the Papal States, and the Ottoman Empire. His diplomatic efforts helped secure temporary periods of peace and allowed him to maintain a degree of autonomy for the Serbian Despotate.

The Fall of the Serbian Despotate

Despite the efforts of its rulers, the Serbian Despotate faced increasing pressure from the Ottoman Empire. The continued advance of Ottoman forces, combined with internal strife and economic difficulties, ultimately led to the fall of the despotate.

The Fall of Smederevo (1459)

The final blow to the Serbian Despotate came in 1459, when the Ottomans captured the fortress of Smederevo, the last stronghold of the despotate. The fall of Smederevo marked the end of the Serbian Despotate and the complete incorporation of Serbian territories into the Ottoman Empire.

1. **Economic Decline**: The continuous warfare and tribute payments to the Ottomans strained the economy of the Serbian Despotate. The economic decline weakened the despotate's ability to sustain its military and administrative structures.
2. **Internal Strife**: Internal conflicts and power struggles among the nobility further weakened the despotate. The lack of a unified leadership made it difficult to mount an effective defense against the Ottoman advances.

Legacy of the Serbian Despotate

The Serbian Despotate, despite its struggles and ultimate fall, left a lasting legacy in Serbian history and culture. The efforts of its rulers to preserve Serbian autonomy, culture, and religious traditions during a period of significant external pressure are noteworthy.

Cultural and Religious Contributions

The cultural and religious contributions of the Serbian Despotate played a crucial role in preserving Serbian identity and heritage. The support for monasticism, the construction of religious institutions, and the patronage of the arts ensured the continuity of Serbian cultural traditions.

1. **Monasteries and Churches**: The monasteries and churches built during this period, such as Manasija and Ravanica, remain important cultural and historical sites. These institutions were centers of learning, artistic production, and religious life, contributing to the preservation of Serbian heritage.

2. **Literary Achievements**: The literary achievements of rulers like Stefan Lazarević enriched Serbian literature and provided a record of the period's cultural and intellectual life. Works like "Slovo ljubve" continue to be celebrated as important contributions to Serbian literature.

Resistance and Resilience

The resistance and resilience demonstrated by the Serbian Despotate in the face of Ottoman expansion are remembered as significant aspects of Serbian history. The defense of Belgrade and the efforts to maintain autonomy in a challenging political landscape reflect the determination and courage of its leaders.

Conclusion: The End of Medieval Serbia

The fall of the Serbian Despotate in 1459 marked the end of medieval Serbia and the beginning of a long period of Ottoman rule. The struggles and achievements of the despotate's rulers highlight the complexities and challenges of maintaining sovereignty in a rapidly changing political environment.

As we continue our exploration of Serbian history, we will examine the impact of Ottoman rule on Serbian society, culture, and identity. The legacy of the Serbian Despotate, with its cultural contributions and resistance efforts, provides valuable insights into the resilience and enduring spirit of the Serbian people. Despite the fall of their medieval state, the foundations laid during this period continued to influence and shape Serbian identity and heritage in the centuries to come.

Chapter 13: The Ottoman Rule and the Serbian Resistance

The fall of the Serbian Despotate in 1459 marked the beginning of nearly five centuries of Ottoman rule over Serbian territories. This period was characterized by significant changes in political, social, and economic structures, as well as continuous resistance and efforts to preserve Serbian cultural and religious identity. This chapter explores the complexities of Ottoman rule in Serbia, the various forms of resistance that emerged, and the enduring spirit of the Serbian people during this challenging era.

The Establishment of Ottoman Rule

The Conquest and Administrative Changes

Following the fall of the Serbian Despotate, the Ottomans rapidly consolidated their control over Serbian territories. They implemented a well-organized administrative system to govern the newly acquired lands, integrating them into the broader Ottoman Empire.

1. **Timar System**: The Ottomans introduced the timar system, a form of feudal land tenure, where land was granted to military officers (sipahis) in exchange for their service. This system helped ensure loyalty to the Ottoman Sultan and facilitated efficient tax collection and military recruitment.

2. **Millet System**: The millet system allowed for a degree of religious autonomy among the empire's diverse populations. The Serbian Orthodox Church was placed under the jurisdiction of the Patriarchate of Constantinople, but local churches and monasteries retained some autonomy in

religious affairs.

3. **Administrative Divisions**: Serbian territories were divided into sanjaks (administrative districts) and vilayets (provinces), each governed by an Ottoman-appointed official. These divisions helped integrate the region into the empire's administrative framework.

Economic Impact

The Ottoman conquest brought significant changes to the Serbian economy. The new administrative and land tenure systems, combined with heavy taxation, had profound effects on agricultural production, trade, and overall economic stability.

1. **Taxation**: The Ottomans imposed various taxes on the Serbian population, including the poll tax (jizya) on non-Muslims. These taxes placed a heavy burden on peasants and landowners, leading to economic hardship and social discontent.

2. **Agricultural Production**: The timar system disrupted traditional agricultural practices, as sipahis often prioritized short-term gains over sustainable farming. This led to fluctuations in agricultural productivity and affected food security.

3. **Trade and Commerce**: While the Ottomans established trade routes that connected Serbian territories with other parts of the empire, the local economy struggled due to the heavy taxation and exploitation by Ottoman officials.

Forms of Serbian Resistance

Despite the challenges posed by Ottoman rule, the Serbian people continually sought ways to resist and preserve their cultural and religious identity. Resistance took various forms, from armed uprisings to cultural preservation and religious defiance.

Armed Rebellions

Throughout the Ottoman period, there were numerous armed rebellions and uprisings led by Serbian nobles, peasants, and religious leaders. These uprisings were often fueled by economic hardship, heavy taxation, and a desire for independence.

1. **The Uprising of 1594**: One of the significant uprisings occurred in 1594, led by the Serbian Patriarch Jovan Kantul and local nobles. The rebellion was part of the broader Long Turkish War (1593-1606) between the Habsburg Monarchy and the Ottoman Empire. Despite initial successes, the rebellion was ultimately crushed by the Ottomans.

2. **The First Serbian Uprising (1804-1813)**: The First Serbian Uprising, led by Karađorđe Petrović, marked a major turning point in Serbian resistance against Ottoman rule. Beginning in 1804, the uprising sought to establish an independent Serbian state. Although it was suppressed by the Ottomans in 1813, it laid the groundwork for subsequent efforts towards independence.

3. **The Second Serbian Uprising (1815-1817)**: The Second Serbian Uprising, led by Miloš Obrenović, succeeded in securing autonomy for Serbia within the Ottoman Empire. The uprising began in 1815 and resulted in the establishment of the Principality of Serbia, which enjoyed a degree of self-governance under Ottoman suzerainty.

Cultural and Religious Resistance

In addition to armed rebellions, the Serbian people engaged in cultural and religious resistance to preserve their identity and heritage.

1. **The Role of the Serbian Orthodox Church**: The Serbian Orthodox Church played a crucial role in maintaining cultural and religious continuity. Monasteries and churches served as centers of education, cultural preservation, and resistance. The church helped preserve the Serbian language, traditions, and historical memory through religious texts, liturgical practices, and folklore.

2. **Cultural Preservation**: Serbian folklore, epic poetry, and oral traditions became vital tools for preserving national identity and history. Epic poems, such as those recounting the Battle of Kosovo, kept the memory of Serbian heroes and martyrs alive, fostering a sense of national pride and resistance.

3. **Education and Scholarship**: Despite the restrictions imposed by Ottoman rule, Serbian scholars and clergy continued to pursue education and scholarship. Monasteries such as Hilandar on Mount Athos remained important centers of learning and manuscript production, preserving Serbian literary and religious traditions.

The Impact of Ottoman Rule on Serbian Society

The long period of Ottoman rule had profound effects on various aspects of Serbian society, including social structures, religious life, and cultural development.

Social Structures

1. **Peasantry and Land Ownership**: The Ottoman land tenure system significantly affected the Serbian peasantry. Many peasants became tenant farmers, working the land for sipahis

and paying high taxes and rents. This system led to widespread poverty and social unrest.

2. **Urbanization and Trade**: Ottoman rule brought changes to urbanization and trade patterns. While some cities, such as Belgrade, grew as trade centers, others declined due to economic exploitation and administrative neglect. The Ottoman influence introduced new architectural styles, markets, and trade practices.

3. **Social Hierarchies**: The social hierarchy under Ottoman rule was characterized by a clear distinction between Muslims and non-Muslims. Non-Muslims, including Serbs, were subject to various restrictions and discriminations, impacting their social mobility and opportunities.

Religious Life

1. **Religious Autonomy and Restrictions**: While the millet system allowed for a degree of religious autonomy, the Serbian Orthodox Church faced restrictions and pressures. The church had to navigate a complex relationship with the Ottoman authorities, balancing cooperation with the preservation of its traditions and autonomy.

2. **Monastic Life**: Monastic communities played a vital role in maintaining religious and cultural continuity. Monasteries such as Studenica, Dečani, and Mileševa continued to function as centers of spiritual life, education, and cultural preservation despite the challenges posed by Ottoman rule.

3. **Religious Persecution and Conversion**: The Ottoman policy of religious tolerance was often inconsistently applied. Instances of religious persecution and forced conversions to Islam occurred, particularly during periods of conflict and rebellion. However, many Serbs remained steadfast in their faith, viewing their religious identity as integral to their

resistance.

The Path to Autonomy and Independence

The continuous resistance efforts and changing geopolitical dynamics eventually paved the way for Serbian autonomy and independence in the 19th century.

The Role of European Powers

The weakening of the Ottoman Empire and the rise of European powers played a significant role in the Serbian struggle for independence. The involvement of Russia, Austria, and other European states provided crucial support for Serbian aspirations.

1. **Russian Support**: Russia, as a fellow Orthodox Christian nation, supported the Serbian cause diplomatically and militarily. Russian influence was instrumental in the recognition of Serbian autonomy and later independence.
2. **Austrian Influence**: Austria also played a role in the Serbian struggle for independence, particularly during the wars with the Ottoman Empire. Austrian support helped bolster Serbian resistance efforts and provided a counterbalance to Ottoman power.
3. **International Diplomacy**: The broader context of European diplomacy and the decline of the Ottoman Empire created opportunities for Serbian leaders to negotiate autonomy and independence. The Congress of Berlin in 1878 formally recognized the independence of the Principality of Serbia.

The Rise of National Movements

The 19th century saw the rise of national movements across Europe, including the Serbian national movement, which sought to revive and promote Serbian identity, culture, and statehood.

1. **Vuk Karadžić and Language Reform**: Vuk Karadžić, a prominent Serbian linguist and reformer, played a crucial role in the standardization and preservation of the Serbian language. His efforts to collect and publish Serbian folk tales, epic poetry, and linguistic studies contributed to the national awakening.

2. **Educational and Cultural Initiatives**: The establishment of educational institutions, cultural societies, and literary circles helped promote Serbian national consciousness. These initiatives fostered a sense of unity and identity among Serbs, laying the groundwork for political and social reforms.

3. **Political Leadership**: Leaders such as Miloš Obrenović and later Prince Alexander Karađorđević navigated the complex political landscape to secure autonomy and independence for Serbia. Their leadership and diplomatic efforts were instrumental in achieving Serbian statehood.

Conclusion: Enduring Spirit and Identity

The period of Ottoman rule in Serbia was marked by significant challenges, but it also demonstrated the resilience and enduring spirit of the Serbian people. Through armed resistance, cultural preservation, and religious defiance, the Serbs maintained their identity and laid the foundation for future independence.

As we continue our exploration of Serbian history, we will examine the efforts to rebuild and modernize the Serbian state in the 19th and early 20th centuries. The legacies of the Ottoman period, with its complex interactions between rulers and the ruled, resistance and accommodation, continue to shape the Serbian national consciousness and historical memory. Despite centuries of foreign domination, the Serbian people preserved their cultural and religious heritage, ultimately emerging as an independent nation with a strong sense of identity and pride.

Chapter 14: Milos Obrenović and the Formation of Modern Serbia

The early 19th century marked a pivotal period in Serbian history as the nation began its transition from centuries of Ottoman rule to the establishment of a modern state. Central to this transformation was Milos Obrenović, a key leader in the Serbian struggle for autonomy and the founder of the modern Serbian state. This chapter explores the life and reign of Milos Obrenović, his role in the Serbian uprisings, the establishment of the Principality of Serbia, and his efforts to modernize the nation.

Early Life and Background

Milos Obrenović was born on March 18, 1780, in the village of Brusnica, near Požega, in central Serbia. He was born into a peasant family, the Obrenovićs, and his early life was marked by the hardships and challenges faced by many Serbs under Ottoman rule. Despite his humble beginnings, Milos displayed leadership qualities and an astute understanding of politics and military strategy from a young age.

Early Career and Rise to Prominence

Milos Obrenović first rose to prominence during the First Serbian Uprising (1804-1813) against Ottoman rule. The uprising was led by Karađorđe Petrović, and Milos quickly distinguished himself as a capable military leader and strategist. He fought alongside other Serbian leaders in various battles, contributing to the early successes of the rebellion.

When the First Serbian Uprising was eventually suppressed by the Ottomans in 1813, Milos retreated to the hills with a group of loyal followers. Despite the defeat, he remained committed to the cause of Serbian autonomy and began planning for future resistance.

The Second Serbian Uprising (1815-1817)

The Second Serbian Uprising, led by Milos Obrenović, began in April 1815. This rebellion was more organized and strategically planned than the first, benefiting from the lessons learned during the previous uprising.

Outbreak of the Uprising

The Second Serbian Uprising was sparked by the harsh treatment of Serbs by Ottoman officials and the desire for greater autonomy. Milos Obrenović emerged as the natural leader of the rebellion, rallying support from various regions and organizing the resistance.

1. **Strategic Leadership**: Milos demonstrated remarkable strategic acumen, coordinating attacks on Ottoman garrisons and effectively utilizing guerrilla warfare tactics. His leadership inspired confidence and unity among the Serbian fighters.
2. **Diplomatic Efforts**: Milos also engaged in diplomatic efforts to secure support from European powers. He communicated with representatives of the Russian Empire and other potential allies, seeking to gain international backing for the Serbian cause.

Key Battles and Successes

The Second Serbian Uprising saw several significant battles and successes that helped pave the way for Serbian autonomy.

1. **Battle of Dublje**: One of the notable battles of the uprising was the Battle of Dublje, fought in July 1815. Milos Obrenović's forces achieved a decisive victory against the Ottomans, boosting morale and gaining control over key territories.
2. **Siege of Belgrade**: The successful siege and eventual capture of Belgrade in 1817 was a turning point in the uprising. The fall of Belgrade to Serbian forces demonstrated the effectiveness of the rebellion and pressured the Ottoman authorities to negotiate.

The Establishment of the Principality of Serbia

The successes of the Second Serbian Uprising and Milos Obrenović's leadership led to significant political changes. In 1817, the Ottoman authorities, recognizing the determination and resilience of the Serbian resistance, agreed to negotiate.

The Treaty of Bucharest (1817)

The Treaty of Bucharest, signed in 1817, marked a crucial step towards Serbian autonomy. While the treaty did not grant full independence, it established the Principality of Serbia as an autonomous entity under Ottoman suzerainty. Milos Obrenović was recognized as the hereditary prince (knjaz) of Serbia.

1. **Autonomy and Self-Governance**: The treaty granted the Principality of Serbia a degree of self-governance, allowing for the establishment of Serbian administrative and judicial institutions. This autonomy laid the foundation for the development of a modern Serbian state.
2. **Milos Obrenović as Prince**: Milos Obrenović's position as the hereditary prince solidified his leadership and provided a stable framework for the governance of Serbia. His authority

was recognized by both the Serbian people and the Ottoman authorities.

Reign of Milos Obrenović

As the prince of the autonomous Principality of Serbia, Milos Obrenović embarked on a series of reforms and initiatives aimed at modernizing the nation and strengthening its institutions.

Administrative and Legal Reforms

Milos Obrenović focused on establishing a centralized and efficient administrative system to govern the principality.

1. **Centralization of Power**: Milos centralized power by appointing loyal officials to key positions and reducing the influence of regional leaders. This centralization helped create a cohesive and unified state.
2. **Legal Reforms**: Milos introduced new legal codes that standardized laws across the principality, promoting justice and reducing corruption. These legal reforms were instrumental in creating a stable and predictable legal environment.

Economic Development

Milos Obrenović recognized the importance of economic development for the stability and prosperity of Serbia. His economic policies aimed to promote agriculture, trade, and infrastructure development.

1. **Agricultural Reforms**: Milos implemented agricultural reforms that improved farming techniques and increased productivity. He encouraged the cultivation of new crops and

provided support to farmers, contributing to agricultural growth.

2. **Trade and Commerce**: Milos promoted trade by establishing trade routes and reducing barriers to commerce. He sought to integrate Serbia into regional and international trade networks, enhancing economic opportunities for Serbian merchants.

3. **Infrastructure Development**: Milos invested in infrastructure projects, including the construction of roads, bridges, and public buildings. These improvements facilitated trade and communication, contributing to the overall development of the principality.

Social and Educational Initiatives

Milos Obrenović was committed to improving the social and educational conditions of the Serbian people. His initiatives aimed to enhance literacy, education, and social welfare.

1. **Education Reforms**: Milos established schools and promoted education as a means of fostering a knowledgeable and skilled populace. He encouraged the establishment of primary and secondary schools, as well as vocational training programs.

2. **Cultural and Religious Support**: Milos supported the Serbian Orthodox Church and its cultural initiatives. He funded the restoration and construction of churches and monasteries, promoting religious and cultural continuity.

3. **Social Welfare**: Milos implemented social welfare programs to support vulnerable populations, including orphans and the elderly. His efforts aimed to create a more equitable and just society.

Challenges and Opposition

Despite his achievements, Milos Obrenović faced significant challenges and opposition during his reign. His efforts to centralize power and implement reforms were met with resistance from various quarters.

Internal Opposition

Milos's centralization efforts and authoritative style of governance led to opposition from regional leaders and nobles who sought to maintain their traditional privileges.

1. **Noble Resistance**: Some Serbian nobles resisted Milos's centralization efforts, viewing them as a threat to their autonomy and influence. This resistance occasionally led to conflicts and power struggles.
2. **Political Rivalries**: Milos faced political rivalries and opposition from within his administration. Some officials and leaders sought to undermine his authority and promote their own interests.

External Pressures

Milos Obrenović also had to navigate the complex international landscape, balancing relations with the Ottoman Empire, Russia, and other European powers.

1. **Ottoman Relations**: While the Treaty of Bucharest granted autonomy, Serbia remained under Ottoman suzerainty. Milos had to carefully manage relations with the Ottoman authorities to maintain autonomy while avoiding direct confrontation.
2. **Russian Influence**: Russia, as a supporter of Orthodox Christian nations, provided diplomatic and political support to Serbia. Milos maintained a strategic alliance with Russia,

leveraging this relationship to strengthen Serbia's position.

The Later Years and Legacy of Milos Obrenović

In 1839, facing increasing opposition and pressure, Milos Obrenović abdicated in favor of his son, Milan Obrenović II, who ruled for a short period before being succeeded by his brother, Mihailo Obrenović. However, Milos's legacy continued to shape the future of Serbia.

Return to Power

Milos Obrenović returned to power in 1858, following a period of political instability and the ousting of Prince Alexander Karađorđević. His second reign was marked by efforts to consolidate power and continue his modernization initiatives.

Final Years and Death

Milos Obrenović's final years were spent in efforts to maintain stability and promote development. He died on September 26, 1860, leaving behind a legacy of significant contributions to the formation of modern Serbia.

Legacy and Contributions

Milos Obrenović's legacy is multifaceted, encompassing his role as a leader of the Serbian uprisings, his efforts to establish and govern the Principality of Serbia, and his contributions to modernization and development.

Military and Political Achievements

Milos's leadership during the Second Serbian Uprising and his diplomatic efforts to secure autonomy were pivotal in the establishment of the Principality of Serbia. His centralization of power and administrative reforms laid the foundation for a cohesive and stable state.

Economic and Social Reforms

Milos's economic policies and social initiatives promoted agricultural growth, trade, and education. His efforts to improve infrastructure and support social welfare contributed to the overall development and prosperity of Serbia.

Cultural and Religious Support

Milos's support for the Serbian Orthodox Church and cultural initiatives helped preserve and promote Serbian identity and heritage. His patronage of religious and cultural institutions played a crucial role in fostering a sense of national pride and continuity.

Conclusion: The Architect of Modern Serbia

Milos Obrenović's reign marked a transformative period in Serbian history, characterized by the struggle for autonomy, the establishment of a modern state, and significant efforts towards modernization and development. His leadership, vision, and determination helped lay the foundation for a prosperous and independent Serbia.

As we continue our exploration of Serbian history, we will examine the subsequent efforts to further modernize and strengthen the Serbian state in the late 19th and early 20th centuries. The legacies of Milos Obrenović and other key figures in Serbian history provide valuable insights into the evolution of the nation and its enduring spirit of resilience and progress. Despite the challenges and complexities of their times, these leaders contributed to the formation of a vibrant and dynamic Serbian state, shaping its path towards a brighter future.

Chapter 15: Mihailo Obrenović and the Path to Independence

Following the foundational work of Milos Obrenović, the task of further modernizing and securing Serbia's independence fell to his son, Mihailo Obrenović. Mihailo's reigns, first briefly from 1839 to 1842 and then more definitively from 1860 to 1868, were marked by significant political, economic, and military efforts aimed at strengthening the Serbian state and securing its autonomy from the Ottoman Empire. This chapter explores the life and reign of Mihailo Obrenović, his policies, and the lasting impact of his efforts on the path to Serbian independence.

Early Life and First Reign

Mihailo Obrenović was born on September 16, 1823, in Kragujevac, Serbia. As the second son of Milos Obrenović, he grew up in a politically charged environment, witnessing his father's struggles and achievements in the fight for Serbian autonomy.

Ascension to the Throne

In 1839, after the abdication of Milos Obrenović, Mihailo's elder brother, Milan Obrenović II, briefly became prince but died shortly thereafter. Mihailo, at the age of 16, then ascended to the throne. His first reign was marked by political instability and internal opposition, leading to his eventual deposition in 1842.

Political Challenges

Mihailo's early reign faced significant challenges from various factions within Serbia. The Karađorđević family, rivals of·the Obrenovićs, capitalized on Mihailo's youth and inexperience, leading a successful coup that resulted in the ascension of Alexander Karađorđević. Mihailo went into exile, spending the next several years in Western Europe, where he observed modern political and military systems, which influenced his later reforms.

Return to Power and Second Reign

In 1858, political dynamics in Serbia shifted again, and Milos Obrenović was restored to power. Following Milos's death in 1860, Mihailo returned to the throne. His second reign was marked by a more mature and strategic approach to governance, focusing on modernization and securing independence.

Modernization Efforts

Mihailo Obrenović implemented a series of reforms aimed at modernizing Serbia and preparing it for future independence.

1. **Administrative Reforms**: Mihailo reorganized the administrative structure of Serbia, aiming to create a more efficient and centralized government. He appointed competent officials and reduced the influence of regional leaders who had previously undermined central authority.
2. **Legal Reforms**: Mihailo introduced new legal codes to standardize laws and promote justice. These reforms included the establishment of modern courts and legal procedures, contributing to a more predictable and fair legal environment.
3. **Economic Development**: Recognizing the importance of economic stability, Mihailo focused on promoting trade, agriculture, and industry. He encouraged the development of infrastructure, including roads and railways, to facilitate

commerce and communication.

Military Reforms

One of Mihailo's key priorities was to strengthen the Serbian military in preparation for the eventual struggle for full independence.

1. **Modernization of the Army**: Mihailo reformed the Serbian army, introducing modern training techniques and military organization. He sought to build a professional and disciplined force capable of defending the nation.
2. **Establishment of a National Militia**: In addition to the regular army, Mihailo established a national militia to serve as a reserve force. This militia provided additional manpower and ensured that a large portion of the population was prepared for military service.
3. **Diplomatic and Military Alliances**: Mihailo pursued alliances with other Balkan states, recognizing the importance of regional cooperation against the Ottoman Empire. He engaged in diplomatic efforts to build a coalition that could support Serbia's aspirations for independence.

The Quest for Independence

Mihailo Obrenović's reign was characterized by strategic efforts to secure Serbia's independence from the Ottoman Empire. His diplomatic and military initiatives were aimed at creating favorable conditions for an eventual break from Ottoman control.

Diplomatic Initiatives

Mihailo engaged in extensive diplomatic efforts to gain support for Serbia's independence. He established strong ties with Russia, Austria, and other European powers, seeking their backing for Serbia's national aspirations.

1. **Alliance with Russia**: Russia, as a fellow Orthodox Christian nation and a long-time supporter of Balkan independence movements, was a crucial ally for Serbia. Mihailo's diplomatic efforts strengthened this alliance, ensuring Russian support for Serbia's cause.

2. **Balkan League**: Mihailo worked to create a Balkan League, a coalition of Balkan states united against the Ottoman Empire. He held discussions with leaders from Montenegro, Greece, and Bulgaria, promoting the idea of a coordinated effort for independence.

3. **European Diplomacy**: Mihailo also engaged in diplomacy with Western European powers, including Austria and France. He sought to present Serbia as a modernizing state deserving of international support and recognition.

Military Preparations

Mihailo's military preparations were aimed at building a capable and modern army that could effectively challenge Ottoman authority when the time came.

1. **Training and Equipment**: Mihailo invested in modern military training and equipment, ensuring that the Serbian army was well-prepared and equipped. He sent officers abroad to study military techniques and brought foreign military advisors to Serbia.

2. **Fortifications and Defense**: Mihailo strengthened Serbia's defenses by building fortifications and improving existing

military infrastructure. Key strategic points were fortified to provide a strong defense against potential Ottoman attacks.

Cultural and Educational Reforms

Mihailo Obrenović understood that building a strong national identity and educated populace was essential for the success of his modernization efforts and the future independence of Serbia.

Educational Reforms

Mihailo implemented significant reforms in the education sector to promote literacy and knowledge among the Serbian population.

1. **Establishment of Schools**: Mihailo expanded the network of primary and secondary schools across Serbia. He emphasized the importance of education for all social classes and promoted the establishment of public schools.
2. **Higher Education**: Mihailo supported the development of higher education institutions, including the University of Belgrade. He recognized the need for a well-educated elite to lead the nation and contribute to its modernization.
3. **Curriculum Development**: Educational reforms included the development of a modern curriculum that emphasized science, mathematics, and technical skills, along with traditional subjects. This curriculum aimed to prepare students for the challenges of a modern state.

Cultural Patronage

Mihailo was a patron of the arts and culture, supporting various initiatives that promoted Serbian heritage and national identity.

1. **Literature and Arts**: Mihailo supported Serbian writers,

poets, and artists, providing them with the resources and platforms to create and share their work. He recognized the importance of cultural expression in building a strong national identity.

2. **Cultural Institutions**: Mihailo funded the establishment of cultural institutions, including theaters, libraries, and museums. These institutions played a crucial role in preserving and promoting Serbian culture and history.

3. **Historical Commemoration**: Mihailo promoted the commemoration of significant events and figures in Serbian history. He supported the creation of monuments and memorials that honored the contributions of Serbian heroes and martyrs.

Challenges and Opposition

Despite his numerous achievements, Mihailo Obrenović faced significant challenges and opposition during his reign.

Internal Opposition

Mihailo's efforts to centralize power and implement reforms were met with resistance from various factions within Serbia.

1. **Noble Resistance**: Some Serbian nobles resisted Mihailo's centralization efforts, viewing them as a threat to their traditional privileges and autonomy. This resistance occasionally led to conflicts and political rivalries.

2. **Political Rivalries**: Mihailo faced opposition from political rivals, including members of the Karađorđević family and other influential leaders. These rivalries often created instability and challenges to his authority.

External Pressures

Mihailo's foreign policy and military preparations brought him into conflict with the Ottoman Empire and other regional powers.

1. **Ottoman Hostility**: The Ottoman authorities viewed Mihailo's efforts to build alliances and strengthen the Serbian military as a direct threat. Tensions between Serbia and the Ottoman Empire increased, leading to periodic conflicts and diplomatic strains.

2. **Regional Tensions**: Mihailo's efforts to create a Balkan League were met with mixed reactions from neighboring states. While some leaders supported the idea, others were cautious about forming alliances that might provoke Ottoman retaliation.

Assassination and Legacy

Mihailo Obrenović's efforts to modernize and strengthen Serbia were tragically cut short by his assassination in 1868. His death marked a significant loss for the nation, but his legacy continued to shape Serbia's path towards independence.

Assassination

On June 10, 1868, Mihailo Obrenović was assassinated while riding in a carriage in Košutnjak, a park near Belgrade. The assassination was carried out by a group of conspirators with political motives, likely linked to his internal opposition and rivalries.

Legacy

Mihailo Obrenović's legacy is profound and multifaceted. His reign marked a critical period in Serbian history, characterized by significant efforts towards modernization, military strengthening, and the pursuit of independence.

1. **Modernization and Reforms**: Mihailo's administrative, legal, and economic reforms laid the foundation for a modern Serbian state. His efforts to centralize power, promote education, and develop infrastructure were crucial for the nation's progress.

2. **Military Preparedness**: Mihailo's military reforms and preparations significantly strengthened the Serbian army, making it a more capable and professional force. His efforts ensured that Serbia was better prepared for future conflicts and struggles for independence.

3. **Cultural and Educational Contributions**: Mihailo's support for education, culture, and national identity played a vital role in fostering a sense of unity and pride among the Serbian people. His cultural patronage and educational initiatives helped preserve and promote Serbian heritage.

4. **Path to Independence**: While Mihailo did not live to see Serbia's full independence, his efforts significantly advanced the nation's progress towards autonomy. His diplomatic and military initiatives laid the groundwork for future leaders to continue the struggle for independence.

Conclusion: A Pivotal Leader in Serbian History

Mihailo Obrenović's reign represents a pivotal period in Serbian history, marked by significant efforts towards modernization, military strengthening, and the pursuit of independence. His leadership, vision, and determination helped lay the foundation for a prosperous and independent Serbia.

As we continue our exploration of Serbian history, we will examine the subsequent efforts to achieve full independence and the challenges faced by the nation in the late 19th and early 20th centuries. The legacies of Mihailo Obrenović and other key figures in Serbian history provide valuable insights into the evolution of the nation and its enduring spirit of resilience and progress. Despite the challenges and complexities of their times, these leaders contributed to the formation of a vibrant and dynamic Serbian state, shaping its path towards a brighter future.

Chapter 16: The Road to Full Independence: Serbia in the Late 19th Century

Following the reign of Mihailo Obrenović, Serbia continued its journey towards full independence. The late 19th century was a transformative period marked by significant political, social, and economic changes. Key events during this period included the formal recognition of Serbian independence, efforts to modernize the state, and the complexities of balancing regional and international relations. This chapter explores Serbia's path to full independence, highlighting the crucial moments and figures that shaped its destiny.

The Reign of Milan Obrenović IV (1868-1889)

After the assassination of Mihailo Obrenović, the Serbian throne passed to his cousin, Milan Obrenović IV. Milan's reign was marked by efforts to consolidate Serbia's autonomy and secure its recognition as a fully independent state.

Early Reign and Challenges

Milan Obrenović IV ascended to the throne at the age of 14, necessitating a regency until he reached maturity. The early years of his reign were characterized by political instability and the need to address internal and external challenges.

1. **Regency Period**: During Milan's minority, a regency council governed Serbia. This period was marked by efforts to stabilize the government and address the political factions that had emerged following Mihailo's assassination.

2. **Internal Reforms**: Upon reaching maturity, Milan undertook several internal reforms to strengthen the state's administrative and military capabilities. These reforms included modernizing the army, improving infrastructure, and promoting economic development.

The Serbian-Turkish Wars (1876-1878)

One of the most significant events during Milan's reign was the Serbian-Turkish Wars, which played a crucial role in the path to full independence.

1. **First Serbian-Turkish War (1876-1877)**: The first conflict began in 1876, as Serbia declared war on the Ottoman Empire, seeking to capitalize on the weakening Ottoman control in the Balkans. Despite initial setbacks, the conflict highlighted Serbia's determination to achieve full independence.
2. **Second Serbian-Turkish War (1877-1878)**: The second conflict, part of the broader Russo-Turkish War, saw Serbia align with Russia against the Ottomans. The Serbian army achieved significant victories, capturing key territories and demonstrating its military capabilities.

The Treaty of Berlin (1878)

The conclusion of the Russo-Turkish War and the subsequent Treaty of Berlin in 1878 were pivotal for Serbia's international status.

1. **International Recognition**: The Treaty of Berlin formally recognized the independence of the Principality of Serbia. This recognition was a significant milestone, affirming Serbia's status as a sovereign state and ending its vassalage to the Ottoman Empire.

2. **Territorial Gains**: The treaty also granted Serbia additional territories, including Niš, Pirot, and Vranje, expanding its borders and enhancing its strategic position in the Balkans.

The Reign of Aleksandar Obrenović (1889-1903)

Following Milan's abdication in 1889, his son, Aleksandar Obrenović, ascended to the throne. Aleksandar's reign was marked by efforts to further modernize Serbia and navigate the complexities of regional politics.

Early Reign and Modernization

Aleksandar Obrenović sought to continue the modernization efforts initiated by his predecessors. His reign was characterized by significant political and economic reforms.

1. **Constitutional Reforms**: In 1889, Aleksandar enacted a new constitution, which aimed to balance the powers of the monarchy and the parliament. This constitution provided a framework for democratic governance and the protection of civil liberties.
2. **Economic Development**: Aleksandar focused on promoting industrialization and economic growth. His policies included the development of infrastructure, such as railways and telegraph lines, and the promotion of foreign investment in Serbian industries.

Political Instability and Opposition

Despite his modernization efforts, Aleksandar's reign faced significant political instability and opposition from various factions.

1. **Authoritarian Tendencies**: Aleksandar's tendency towards

authoritarian rule and his frequent interference in parliamentary affairs led to tensions with political leaders and the public. His actions undermined the democratic principles established by the constitution.

2. **Military Coup (1903)**: The growing dissatisfaction with Aleksandar's rule culminated in a military coup in 1903. Aleksandar and his wife, Queen Draga, were assassinated, leading to the end of the Obrenović dynasty. The coup was a turning point in Serbian history, reflecting the deep political divisions and the desire for change.

The Reign of Peter I Karađorđević (1903-1921)

Following the coup, Peter I Karađorđević, a descendant of the leader of the First Serbian Uprising, ascended to the throne. Peter's reign marked a new chapter in Serbian history, characterized by efforts to further democratize the state and secure its position in the Balkans.

Democratic Reforms and National Unity

Peter I Karađorđević's reign was marked by significant efforts to promote democratic governance and national unity.

1. **Constitutional Monarchy**: Peter I reaffirmed the principles of constitutional monarchy, respecting the role of the parliament and promoting political pluralism. His commitment to democratic governance helped stabilize the political landscape and fostered a sense of national unity.

2. **Social and Economic Reforms**: Peter I implemented social and economic reforms aimed at improving the living conditions of the Serbian people. These reforms included land redistribution, support for education, and the development of healthcare services.

The Balkan Wars (1912-1913)

The Balkan Wars were a critical period in Serbian history, as the nation sought to expand its territory and assert its influence in the region.

1. **First Balkan War (1912-1913)**: In the First Balkan War, Serbia joined the Balkan League, an alliance with Montenegro, Greece, and Bulgaria, to fight against the Ottoman Empire. The war resulted in significant territorial gains for Serbia, including Kosovo and parts of Macedonia.
2. **Second Balkan War (1913)**: The Second Balkan War saw Serbia and its allies fight against Bulgaria over the division of the territories gained in the First Balkan War. Serbia emerged victorious, further consolidating its territorial gains and strengthening its position in the Balkans.

World War I and Its Aftermath

World War I was a transformative period for Serbia, marked by immense sacrifice and significant geopolitical changes.

The Outbreak of War

The assassination of Archduke Franz Ferdinand of Austria-Hungary in Sarajevo in 1914 set off a chain of events that led to the outbreak of World War I. Serbia found itself at the center of the conflict, facing an invasion by Austro-Hungarian forces.

1. **Initial Invasions**: Serbia successfully repelled the initial Austro-Hungarian invasions in 1914, achieving notable victories at the battles of Cer and Kolubara. These victories bolstered Serbian morale and demonstrated the resilience of its military forces.
2. **Occupation and Hardship**: Despite early successes, Serbia

was eventually occupied by the Central Powers in 1915. The occupation brought immense suffering, with widespread destruction, famine, and disease affecting the Serbian population.

The Serbian Army's Retreat and Recovery

One of the most dramatic episodes of World War I for Serbia was the retreat of the Serbian army through Albania to the Greek island of Corfu.

1. **The Great Retreat**: Facing overwhelming enemy forces, the Serbian army, along with the civilian population, embarked on a grueling retreat across the mountains of Albania in the winter of 1915-1916. Despite the harsh conditions and heavy losses, the retreat allowed the Serbian army to regroup and recover.

2. **Reorganization and Allied Support**: On Corfu, the Serbian army reorganized and received support from Allied forces. The reinvigorated Serbian army later played a crucial role in the Salonika Front, contributing to the eventual defeat of the Central Powers in the Balkans.

Post-War Reconstruction and the Formation of Yugoslavia

The end of World War I brought significant changes to the political landscape of the Balkans and the formation of a new state.

1. **Territorial Gains**: Following the war, Serbia emerged as a victor and gained additional territories, including parts of Vojvodina, Bosnia and Herzegovina, and Croatia.

2. **Formation of Yugoslavia**: In December 1918, the Kingdom of Serbs, Croats, and Slovenes (later known as Yugoslavia) was established, uniting various South Slavic peoples under

a single state. Peter I Karađorđević became the first king of the new kingdom, marking the culmination of Serbia's efforts towards national unity and independence.

Legacy and Contributions

The late 19th and early 20th centuries were transformative periods in Serbian history, marked by significant achievements and challenges.

Achievements

1. **Independence and Sovereignty**: Serbia successfully achieved and secured its independence from the Ottoman Empire, establishing itself as a sovereign state recognized by the international community.
2. **Modernization and Reforms**: The period saw significant modernization efforts, including administrative, legal, economic, and social reforms that laid the foundation for a modern Serbian state.
3. **Territorial Expansion**: Through the Balkan Wars and World War I, Serbia expanded its territories and strengthened its strategic position in the Balkans.

Challenges

1. **Political Instability**: The period was marked by political instability, including internal opposition, coups, and assassinations. These challenges highlighted the complexities of governance and the need for effective leadership.
2. **War and Suffering**: The conflicts of the late 19th and early 20th centuries, particularly World War I, brought immense suffering to the Serbian population. The hardships faced during these wars had lasting social and economic impacts.

Conclusion: The Path to a New Nation

The late 19th and early 20th centuries were pivotal in shaping modern Serbia. The efforts of leaders like Milan and Aleksandar Obrenović, and later Peter I Karađorđević, played crucial roles in securing independence, promoting modernization, and achieving national unity. Despite the challenges and hardships, Serbia emerged as a sovereign state with a strong sense of national identity.

As we continue our exploration of Serbian history, we will examine the subsequent developments in the Kingdom of Yugoslavia, the complexities of the interwar period, and the challenges faced during World War II. The legacies of this transformative period provide valuable insights into the resilience and determination of the Serbian people, as they navigated the path towards independence and modernity. The achievements and struggles of this era laid the groundwork for the future development and progress of the Serbian nation.

Chapter 17: The Kingdom of Yugoslavia: Unity and Division

Following the end of World War I and the formation of the Kingdom of Serbs, Croats, and Slovenes in 1918, the newly established state sought to unify various South Slavic peoples under a single national identity. This chapter explores the complexities of the Kingdom of Yugoslavia, from its formation to the interwar period and the challenges of governance, national unity, and external pressures.

Formation of the Kingdom of Serbs, Croats, and Slovenes

The end of World War I brought significant geopolitical changes to the Balkans. The collapse of the Austro-Hungarian Empire and the Ottoman Empire created a power vacuum that South Slavic leaders sought to fill with a unified state.

The Corfu Declaration

The Corfu Declaration, signed on July 20, 1917, was a pivotal agreement between the Kingdom of Serbia and the Yugoslav Committee, which represented South Slavic groups from Austria-Hungary. The declaration laid the groundwork for the creation of a unified South Slavic state.

1. **Key Provisions**: The Corfu Declaration emphasized the establishment of a constitutional monarchy under the Serbian royal family, with equal rights for all nationalities and religions within the new state.

2. **International Support**: The declaration garnered support from the Allied powers, who saw the formation of a unified

South Slavic state as a means to stabilize the Balkans and counterbalance the influence of other regional powers.

Proclamation of the Kingdom

On December 1, 1918, the Kingdom of Serbs, Croats, and Slovenes was officially proclaimed. The new kingdom was led by King Peter I of Serbia, with his son, Regent Alexander, playing a significant role in governance.

1. **Territorial Composition**: The kingdom comprised territories from the former Austro-Hungarian Empire (including Croatia, Slovenia, and Bosnia and Herzegovina) and the Kingdom of Serbia (including Vojvodina and Kosovo).
2. **Challenges of Integration**: The integration of diverse ethnic, religious, and cultural groups into a single state posed significant challenges. The new kingdom had to navigate issues of national identity, regional autonomy, and political representation.

Early Governance and Political Tensions

The early years of the Kingdom of Serbs, Croats, and Slovenes were marked by efforts to establish a stable government and address the diverse interests of its constituent groups.

The Vidovdan Constitution

In 1921, the kingdom adopted the Vidovdan Constitution, which established a parliamentary monarchy with a centralized government.

1. **Centralized Authority**: The constitution emphasized a strong central government, reducing the autonomy of individual regions. This centralization was intended to

promote national unity but faced resistance from various ethnic groups.

2. **Political Parties**: The kingdom's political landscape was dominated by parties representing different ethnic and regional interests. The Serbian Radical Party, the Croatian Peasant Party, and the Slovenian People's Party were among the key political actors.

Ethnic and Regional Tensions

The centralized approach to governance led to significant tensions among the kingdom's diverse populations.

1. **Croatian Discontent**: Croatian leaders, particularly from the Croatian Peasant Party, sought greater autonomy and federalism within the kingdom. They resisted the centralizing policies of the Serbian-dominated government.

2. **Slovenian and Bosnian Issues**: Slovenian and Bosnian leaders also faced challenges in balancing their regional interests with the demands of the central government. These tensions often manifested in political conflicts and demands for greater regional rights.

King Alexander's Royal Dictatorship

The growing political instability and ethnic tensions led to a significant shift in governance. In 1929, King Alexander I, who had succeeded his father, proclaimed a royal dictatorship in an attempt to stabilize the kingdom.

Abolition of the Constitution

King Alexander abolished the Vidovdan Constitution and dissolved the parliament, assuming direct control over the government.

1. **Centralization of Power**: The royal dictatorship centralized power in the hands of the king, bypassing the parliamentary system. Alexander aimed to reduce ethnic tensions by promoting a unified Yugoslav identity.
2. **Administrative Reorganization**: The kingdom was reorganized into nine administrative regions (banovinas), designed to weaken ethnic divisions and promote a sense of national unity.

Promoting Yugoslav Identity

King Alexander's policies sought to foster a unified Yugoslav identity that transcended ethnic and regional differences.

1. **Cultural Initiatives**: The government promoted cultural and educational initiatives that emphasized a shared Yugoslav heritage. This included the standardization of the Serbo-Croatian language and the promotion of Yugoslav literature and arts.
2. **Political Repression**: The dictatorship also involved significant political repression. Political parties and organizations that opposed the centralizing policies were banned, and dissent was suppressed.

International Relations and External Pressures

The Kingdom of Yugoslavia faced significant external pressures during the interwar period, navigating complex international relations in a volatile geopolitical landscape.

Relations with Neighboring States

Yugoslavia's relations with its neighbors were shaped by historical animosities and territorial disputes.

1. **Italy and Albania**: Relations with Italy and Albania were particularly tense. Italy harbored ambitions in the Adriatic region and supported Albanian territorial claims against Yugoslavia. This rivalry often led to border skirmishes and diplomatic conflicts.

2. **Hungary and Bulgaria**: Hungary and Bulgaria, both revisionist states seeking to revise the post-World War I borders, posed additional challenges. These states supported separatist movements within Yugoslavia and sought to undermine its territorial integrity.

Alliances and Diplomacy

Yugoslavia sought to secure its position through alliances and diplomatic efforts.

1. **Little Entente**: In the 1920s, Yugoslavia joined the Little Entente, an alliance with Czechoslovakia and Romania aimed at countering Hungarian revisionism and promoting mutual security.

2. **League of Nations**: Yugoslavia was an active member of the League of Nations, advocating for collective security and the resolution of international disputes through diplomacy.

The Assassination of King Alexander and Its Aftermath

King Alexander's efforts to stabilize and unify the kingdom were cut short by his assassination in 1934.

Assassination in Marseille

On October 9, 1934, King Alexander was assassinated in Marseille, France, during an official visit. The assassination was carried out by members of the Internal Macedonian Revolutionary Organization (IMRO) and the Croatian Ustaše, who opposed Alexander's centralizing policies.

1. **International Impact**: The assassination shocked the international community and highlighted the ongoing ethnic and political tensions within Yugoslavia. It also underscored the challenges of maintaining stability in a diverse and divided state.
2. **Succession and Regency**: Following Alexander's assassination, his eleven-year-old son, Peter II, ascended to the throne. A regency council, led by Prince Paul, was established to govern on behalf of the young king.

The Path to World War II

The late 1930s and early 1940s saw Yugoslavia navigate a complex and increasingly dangerous international landscape as Europe moved towards World War II.

Internal Challenges

Yugoslavia continued to face internal challenges, including ethnic tensions and political divisions.

1. **Ethnic Strife**: The centralizing policies of the royal dictatorship had not resolved underlying ethnic tensions. Croatian, Slovenian, and other ethnic groups continued to demand greater autonomy and federalism.
2. **Political Instability**: The regency struggled to maintain political stability, facing opposition from various political factions and separatist movements.

External Pressures and Alliances

The rise of fascist powers in Europe and the looming threat of war placed additional pressures on Yugoslavia.

1. **Axis Powers**: The Axis powers, particularly Nazi Germany and Fascist Italy, sought to expand their influence in the Balkans. Yugoslavia faced increasing pressure to align with the Axis, despite internal opposition to such an alliance.
2. **Tripartite Pact**: In March 1941, under significant pressure, Prince Paul and the Yugoslav government signed the Tripartite Pact, aligning Yugoslavia with the Axis powers. This decision was highly controversial and led to widespread public discontent.

The Coup d'État and the Invasion of Yugoslavia

The signing of the Tripartite Pact sparked a major political crisis and set the stage for dramatic events in Yugoslavia.

The Coup d'État of March 27, 1941

On March 27, 1941, a group of pro-Allied military officers, supported by public opposition to the Axis alignment, carried out a coup d'état. The coup overthrew the regency and brought seventeen-year-old King Peter II to power.

1. **Public Support**: The coup was widely supported by the Serbian population, who viewed it as a rejection of Axis influence and a reaffirmation of Yugoslav sovereignty.
2. **Allied Encouragement**: The coup received encouragement from the Allied powers, particularly the United Kingdom, which sought to counter Axis influence in the Balkans.

The German Invasion

In response to the coup, Nazi Germany, along with its Axis allies, launched an invasion of Yugoslavia on April 6, 1941.

1. **Blitzkrieg Tactics**: The German invasion, employing blitzkrieg tactics, quickly overwhelmed Yugoslav defenses. The Axis forces captured major cities and strategic locations within weeks.
2. **Capitulation and Occupation**: By April 17, 1941, Yugoslavia capitulated, and the country was divided among Axis powers. Germany, Italy, Hungary, and Bulgaria occupied and annexed various regions, while the puppet state of Croatia was established under the Ustaše regime.

The Legacy of the Kingdom of Yugoslavia

The Kingdom of Yugoslavia, despite its brief existence, left a significant legacy in the history of the Balkans and the broader South Slavic region.

Achievements

1. **National Unity**: The kingdom's formation represented a significant attempt to unify diverse South Slavic peoples under a single state. Despite challenges, it laid the groundwork for future efforts towards regional unity.
2. **Modernization**: The kingdom's leaders implemented significant political, economic, and social reforms that modernized the state and improved the living conditions of its people.
3. **International Recognition**: The kingdom achieved international recognition and established itself as a sovereign state, playing an active role in regional and international

diplomacy.

Challenges and Failures

1. **Ethnic Tensions**: The kingdom struggled to reconcile the diverse interests of its constituent ethnic groups, leading to ongoing tensions and conflicts.
2. **Political Instability**: The kingdom faced significant political instability, including coups, assassinations, and authoritarian rule, which undermined its democratic principles.
3. **External Pressures**: The kingdom's geopolitical position made it vulnerable to external pressures from neighboring states and global powers, contributing to its eventual downfall.

Conclusion: The End of an Era

The invasion and occupation of Yugoslavia by Axis forces marked the end of the Kingdom of Yugoslavia and set the stage for a new chapter in the region's history. The legacies of the kingdom's efforts towards unity, modernization, and independence continued to influence the political landscape of the Balkans.

As we continue our exploration of Serbian history, we will examine the impact of World War II on Yugoslavia, the resistance movements, and the post-war establishment of the Socialist Federal Republic of Yugoslavia. The experiences and challenges of the Kingdom of Yugoslavia provide valuable insights into the complexities of nation-building and the enduring quest for unity and stability in the Balkans. Despite its dissolution, the kingdom's legacy remained a significant reference point for future generations in their pursuit of a unified and prosperous South Slavic state.

Chapter 18: World War II and the Yugoslav Resistance

The invasion and occupation of Yugoslavia by Axis powers in April 1941 marked a period of intense struggle, hardship, and resistance. The region, already fraught with ethnic tensions and political instability, became a battleground for opposing ideologies and warring factions. This chapter explores the impact of World War II on Yugoslavia, the emergence of resistance movements, the brutal occupation, and the eventual liberation and reestablishment of the state under a new socialist regime.

The Invasion and Disintegration of Yugoslavia

The swift invasion by Axis forces in April 1941 led to the disintegration of the Kingdom of Yugoslavia. The country was quickly overrun, and its territories were divided among the Axis powers.

The Axis Occupation

Following the invasion, Yugoslavia was partitioned by Germany, Italy, Hungary, and Bulgaria. Each occupying power imposed its own administrative systems and policies, often exacerbating ethnic tensions and fostering brutal repression.

1. **Germany and Italy**: Germany and Italy took control of key strategic areas, with Germany occupying Serbia and establishing a puppet government in Belgrade, while Italy annexed parts of Dalmatia and Montenegro.
2. **Hungary and Bulgaria**: Hungary annexed territories in Vojvodina, while Bulgaria occupied regions in Macedonia and

parts of southern Serbia.

3. **Independent State of Croatia**: The Axis powers established the Independent State of Croatia (NDH), a puppet state governed by the fascist Ustaše regime, led by Ante Pavelić. The NDH included most of modern-day Croatia and Bosnia and Herzegovina.

Brutal Repression and Genocide

The Axis occupation was marked by severe repression, ethnic cleansing, and genocide, particularly under the Ustaše regime in the NDH.

1. **Ustaše Atrocities**: The Ustaše regime implemented policies of ethnic cleansing against Serbs, Jews, and Roma. Concentration camps, such as Jasenovac, became sites of mass murder and brutality. The regime's atrocities led to the deaths of hundreds of thousands of people.

2. **German and Italian Repression**: The German and Italian occupiers also engaged in brutal repression, targeting resistance fighters, civilians, and ethnic groups deemed a threat to their control. Mass executions, forced labor, and deportations were common.

Emergence of Resistance Movements

In response to the brutal occupation, various resistance movements emerged across Yugoslavia, each with different ideologies, goals, and leadership. The two most significant resistance movements were the Partisans, led by Josip Broz Tito, and the Chetniks, led by Draža Mihailović.

The Partisans

The Partisans, officially known as the National Liberation Army and Partisan Detachments of Yugoslavia, were a communist-led resistance movement that sought to liberate Yugoslavia from Axis occupation and establish a socialist state.

1. **Leadership of Josip Broz Tito**: Josip Broz Tito, a charismatic and effective leader, organized and led the Partisans. His leadership was crucial in uniting diverse groups under the Partisan banner and coordinating guerrilla warfare against the Axis occupiers.

2. **Guerrilla Warfare**: The Partisans utilized guerrilla warfare tactics, conducting sabotage operations, ambushes, and hit-and-run attacks on Axis forces. Their knowledge of the local terrain and support from the civilian population were key to their success.

3. **Inclusive Ideology**: The Partisans promoted an inclusive ideology, emphasizing the unity of all Yugoslav ethnic groups in the struggle against fascism. This approach helped garner widespread support from various ethnic communities.

The Chetniks

The Chetniks, officially known as the Yugoslav Army in the Homeland, were a royalist and nationalist resistance movement that aimed to restore the Yugoslav monarchy and protect the Serbian population.

1. **Leadership of Draža Mihailović**: Draža Mihailović, a former Yugoslav army officer, led the Chetniks. His leadership focused on protecting Serb communities from Axis reprisals and seeking support from the Allies for the restoration of the monarchy.

2. **Conflict with Partisans**: Despite a common enemy in the Axis occupiers, the Chetniks and Partisans often found

themselves in conflict. Ideological differences and competition for resources and support led to clashes between the two resistance movements.

3. **Collaboration and Controversy**: The Chetniks' strategy included occasional collaboration with Axis forces against the Partisans, particularly as the war progressed and internal divisions deepened. This collaboration, along with their nationalistic focus, led to controversies and diminished their support.

Key Battles and Campaigns

The resistance movements engaged in numerous significant battles and campaigns throughout the war, contributing to the eventual liberation of Yugoslavia.

Battle of Neretva (1943)

The Battle of Neretva, also known as the Fourth Enemy Offensive, was one of the largest and most significant engagements between the Partisans and Axis forces.

1. **Strategic Importance**: The battle took place in early 1943, as Axis forces sought to destroy the Partisan movement. The Partisans, under Tito's leadership, conducted a strategic retreat across the Neretva River, using innovative tactics to evade and counterattack the Axis forces.

2. **Successful Defense**: Despite being outnumbered and facing difficult terrain, the Partisans successfully defended their positions and inflicted significant casualties on the Axis forces. The battle demonstrated the resilience and tactical prowess of the Partisan movement.

Battle of Sutjeska (1943)

The Battle of Sutjeska, also known as the Fifth Enemy Offensive, was another major engagement that tested the strength and resolve of the Partisan movement.

1. **Encirclement and Breakout**: In mid-1943, Axis forces launched a coordinated offensive to encircle and annihilate the Partisan forces in the Sutjeska region. Tito and his fighters faced overwhelming odds but managed to break through the encirclement and escape to safety.

2. **Heavy Losses**: The battle resulted in heavy losses for the Partisans, including many casualties and the loss of key personnel. However, their ability to survive and continue fighting bolstered their reputation and legitimacy as the leading resistance movement.

Allied Support and Recognition

The international context of World War II played a crucial role in shaping the resistance efforts in Yugoslavia. Both the Partisans and Chetniks sought support from the Allies, but shifting alliances and strategic considerations influenced the level of support each received.

British and American Support

The British and American governments initially supported the Chetniks, viewing them as the legitimate royalist resistance movement. However, reports of Chetnik collaboration with Axis forces and the growing effectiveness of the Partisans led to a shift in Allied support.

1. **Shift to Partisan Support**: By 1943, the Allies recognized the strategic importance and effectiveness of the Partisans. British liaison officers, including the renowned Major Randolph Churchill, were sent to establish direct contact with Tito and his forces.

2. **Supplies and Aid**: The Allies began providing significant supplies, arms, and logistical support to the Partisans. This support included air drops of weapons and equipment, which greatly enhanced the Partisans' capabilities.

Soviet Involvement

The Soviet Union also played a key role in supporting the Partisans, particularly as the Eastern Front progressed and Soviet forces advanced into Eastern Europe.

1. **Coordination and Collaboration**: The Soviets coordinated with the Partisans, providing military support and strategic guidance. Soviet troops later entered Yugoslavia, collaborating with the Partisans in the liberation of key cities and regions.
2. **Political Support**: The Soviet Union's ideological alignment with the Partisans further solidified their support. Tito's vision of a socialist Yugoslavia aligned with Soviet interests, leading to a strong alliance between the Partisans and the Soviet Union.

The Liberation of Yugoslavia

The combined efforts of the Partisan resistance, Allied support, and Soviet intervention culminated in the eventual liberation of Yugoslavia from Axis occupation.

Liberation Campaigns

In 1944 and 1945, the Partisans launched a series of successful offensives to liberate Yugoslav territories from Axis control.

1. **Belgrade Offensive (1944)**: One of the most significant campaigns was the Belgrade Offensive in October 1944. The

Partisans, with support from Soviet troops, successfully liberated Belgrade from German occupation. The victory marked a turning point in the liberation of Yugoslavia.

2. **Final Offensives**: Throughout late 1944 and early 1945, the Partisans continued their offensives, liberating key regions and cities across Yugoslavia. By May 1945, the entire country was liberated from Axis control, and the Partisans emerged as the dominant force in post-war Yugoslavia.

Establishment of the Socialist Federal Republic of Yugoslavia

Following the liberation of Yugoslavia, the Partisans, under Tito's leadership, established a new socialist government, fundamentally transforming the political landscape of the region.

The AVNOJ Conferences

The Anti-Fascist Council for the National Liberation of Yugoslavia (AVNOJ) held several key conferences during the war, laying the groundwork for the post-war government.

1. **Second AVNOJ Conference (1943)**: At the second AVNOJ conference in November 1943, the council declared itself the supreme legislative and executive body of Yugoslavia. The conference also adopted a resolution to establish a federal Yugoslavia composed of six republics: Serbia, Croatia, Slovenia, Bosnia and Herzegovina, Montenegro, and Macedonia.

2. **Third AVNOJ Conference (1945)**: The third AVNOJ conference in April 1945 solidified the decisions made during the war and set the stage for the formal establishment of the Socialist Federal Republic of Yugoslavia (SFRY). The

conference elected Tito as the Prime Minister and Marshal of Yugoslavia.

Post-War Reforms

The new socialist government implemented a series of reforms aimed at rebuilding the country and establishing a socialist state.

1. **Land Reforms**: The government enacted land reforms to redistribute land from large landowners to peasants. These reforms aimed to address social inequalities and promote agricultural productivity.
2. **Industrialization and Nationalization**: The government pursued policies of rapid industrialization and nationalization of key industries. State ownership and central planning were emphasized to drive economic development and modernization.
3. **Social and Cultural Policies**: The new government implemented social policies to improve education, healthcare, and social welfare. Cultural policies promoted Yugoslav unity and socialist ideals, fostering a sense of national identity and solidarity.

Challenges and Legacy

The establishment of the Socialist Federal Republic of Yugoslavia brought both achievements and challenges, shaping the region's future for decades to come.

Achievements

1. **National Unity**: The new government successfully promoted a sense of national unity among the diverse ethnic groups of Yugoslavia. The emphasis on brotherhood and unity helped

mitigate ethnic tensions and foster a shared Yugoslav identity.

2. **Economic Development**: The policies of industrialization and nationalization led to significant economic growth and modernization. Yugoslavia became one of the more developed and industrialized countries in Eastern Europe.

3. **Social Progress**: The government's focus on education, healthcare, and social welfare improved the living standards of the Yugoslav population. Access to education and healthcare expanded, contributing to social progress and equality.

Challenges

1. **Political Repression**: The new socialist government, while achieving significant progress, also engaged in political repression. Opponents of the regime, including former Chetniks and political dissidents, faced persecution and imprisonment.

2. **Ethnic Tensions**: Despite efforts to promote unity, underlying ethnic tensions persisted. The federal structure and centralized policies sometimes exacerbated regional and ethnic grievances.

3. **Cold War Dynamics**: Yugoslavia's unique position as a non-aligned socialist state during the Cold War presented both opportunities and challenges. Balancing relations with the Soviet Union and the Western powers required careful diplomacy and strategic maneuvering.

Conclusion: A New Era for Yugoslavia

The end of World War II and the establishment of the Socialist Federal Republic of Yugoslavia marked the beginning of a new era for the region. The leadership of Josip Broz Tito and the efforts of the Partisan resistance movement fundamentally transformed Yugoslavia, setting it on a path of socialist development and modernization.

As we continue our exploration of Yugoslav history, we will examine the complexities of the post-war period, including the challenges of maintaining unity, the economic and political developments, and the eventual disintegration of Yugoslavia in the late 20th century. The legacy of the wartime resistance and the establishment of the socialist state provide valuable insights into the resilience and adaptability of the Yugoslav people as they navigated the challenges of the 20th century. The experiences of this transformative period continue to shape the region's historical memory and national identities.

Chapter 19: The Socialist Federal Republic of Yugoslavia: Rise and Fall

The Socialist Federal Republic of Yugoslavia (SFRY) emerged from the ashes of World War II as a unique state, navigating the complexities of the Cold War era with a distinctive path of non-alignment and internal federalism. Under the leadership of Josip Broz Tito, Yugoslavia pursued a model of socialist self-management, economic modernization, and ethnic unity. However, the federation also faced numerous challenges that ultimately led to its dissolution in the early 1990s. This chapter explores the rise and fall of the SFRY, examining its political, economic, and social developments, as well as the factors contributing to its disintegration.

Establishment and Early Years of the SFRY

The immediate post-war years were crucial for the consolidation of power by the Yugoslav communists and the establishment of the SFRY.

Tito's Leadership and Policies

Josip Broz Tito emerged as the undisputed leader of post-war Yugoslavia. His leadership style and policies shaped the direction of the new socialist state.

1. **Charismatic Leadership**: Tito's charisma and wartime leadership earned him widespread respect and authority. He was able to unite diverse ethnic groups and maintain stability through a combination of political skill and repressive measures.
2. **Federal Structure**: The SFRY was established as a federation

of six republics: Serbia, Croatia, Slovenia, Bosnia and Herzegovina, Montenegro, and Macedonia. Additionally, Serbia contained two autonomous provinces, Kosovo and Vojvodina. This federal structure aimed to balance the interests of various ethnic groups and regions.

3. **Communist Party Dominance**: The Communist Party of Yugoslavia (later renamed the League of Communists of Yugoslavia) held a monopoly on political power. The party's centralized control was essential for implementing Tito's vision of socialism and maintaining unity.

Economic Reconstruction and Development

The early years of the SFRY focused on reconstructing the war-torn economy and laying the foundation for future development.

1. **Five-Year Plans**: Yugoslavia adopted Soviet-style five-year plans to guide economic development. These plans prioritized heavy industry, infrastructure development, and collectivization of agriculture.

2. **Industrialization**: The government invested heavily in industrialization, building factories, mines, and power plants. This industrial base aimed to transform Yugoslavia into a modern, self-sufficient state.

3. **Land Reforms**: Land reforms were implemented to redistribute land from large landowners to peasants. Collectivization was promoted, although it faced resistance and was less extensive than in the Soviet Union.

Break with the Soviet Union and the Path of Non-Alignment

One of the most significant events in early Yugoslav history was the break with the Soviet Union in 1948, which led to Yugoslavia's unique path of non-alignment.

The Tito-Stalin Split

The Tito-Stalin split marked a turning point in Yugoslav history, as Tito defied Soviet control and pursued an independent path.

1. **Ideological Differences**: The split was driven by ideological and strategic differences between Tito and Stalin. Tito resisted Soviet demands for greater control over Yugoslav affairs, insisting on national sovereignty and independence.
2. **Expulsion from Cominform**: In 1948, Yugoslavia was expelled from the Cominform, the international organization of communist parties led by the Soviet Union. This expulsion isolated Yugoslavia from the Soviet bloc but also allowed it to pursue a more independent course.

Non-Aligned Movement

In response to its isolation from the Soviet bloc, Yugoslavia played a leading role in the formation of the Non-Aligned Movement (NAM).

1. **Founding Member**: Tito, along with leaders such as India's Jawaharlal Nehru and Egypt's Gamal Abdel Nasser, was a founding member of the NAM. The movement sought to provide an alternative to the Cold War superpower blocs, advocating for the independence and sovereignty of newly decolonized nations.
2. **Diplomatic Leadership**: Yugoslavia hosted the first NAM conference in Belgrade in 1961. Tito's leadership in the NAM enhanced Yugoslavia's international standing and provided opportunities for economic and political cooperation with

countries outside the Soviet and Western blocs.

The System of Self-Management

A distinctive feature of Yugoslav socialism was the system of self-management, introduced in the 1950s as an alternative to Soviet-style central planning.

Worker Self-Management

The self-management system aimed to involve workers directly in the management of enterprises and promote economic democracy.

1. **Workers' Councils**: Enterprises were managed by workers' councils, composed of elected representatives of the workforce. These councils had decision-making authority over production, wages, and investment.
2. **Decentralization**: Self-management decentralized economic decision-making, giving greater autonomy to enterprises and reducing the role of central planning. This system aimed to increase efficiency and worker motivation by involving them in management decisions.

Economic Reforms

The self-management system was accompanied by economic reforms designed to modernize the economy and promote growth.

1. **Market Socialism**: Yugoslavia adopted elements of market socialism, allowing for limited market mechanisms within a socialist framework. Prices, wages, and investment decisions were influenced by market conditions, although the state maintained overall control.
2. **Foreign Investment**: The government encouraged foreign

investment and trade, seeking to integrate Yugoslavia into the global economy. This openness to the West contrasted with the more closed economies of other socialist states.

Social and Cultural Developments

The SFRY experienced significant social and cultural changes, as the government promoted education, healthcare, and cultural activities to build a modern socialist society.

Education and Healthcare

Education and healthcare were prioritized as essential components of social development and modernization.

1. **Universal Education**: The government implemented policies to provide universal access to education, from primary school to higher education. Literacy rates improved, and universities expanded, producing a well-educated workforce.
2. **Healthcare System**: A comprehensive healthcare system was established, providing free medical care to all citizens. Investments in healthcare infrastructure and training contributed to improved public health outcomes.

Cultural Policies

The government promoted cultural activities that emphasized socialist values, national unity, and Yugoslav identity.

1. **Cultural Institutions**: The state supported cultural institutions such as theaters, museums, and libraries. Cultural festivals and events celebrated Yugoslav heritage and promoted artistic expression.
2. **Media and Propaganda**: The government controlled the

media, using it to disseminate socialist propaganda and promote national unity. Films, literature, and music were encouraged to reflect socialist ideals and the diversity of Yugoslav culture.

Political Challenges and Internal Tensions

Despite its achievements, the SFRY faced significant political challenges and internal tensions that would ultimately contribute to its disintegration.

Ethnic and Regional Tensions

The federal structure of Yugoslavia, while designed to balance regional interests, also exacerbated ethnic and regional tensions.

1. **Nationalist Movements**: Ethnic nationalism re-emerged as a powerful force, with various groups advocating for greater autonomy or independence. Tensions between Serbs, Croats, Bosniaks, Slovenes, and other groups periodically erupted into political and social conflict.
2. **Economic Disparities**: Economic disparities between the republics contributed to regional tensions. Wealthier republics like Slovenia and Croatia resented the redistribution of resources to poorer regions, while less developed areas felt marginalized and neglected.

Political Reforms and Liberalization

In the 1960s and 1970s, the government implemented political reforms aimed at addressing internal tensions and promoting greater political participation.

1. **Constitutional Changes**: The 1974 constitution granted

greater autonomy to the republics and autonomous provinces, reflecting the growing demands for decentralization. This constitution aimed to balance regional interests but also made the federal system more complex and unwieldy.

2. **Liberalization Efforts**: The government attempted to liberalize the political system by allowing greater freedom of expression and political participation. However, these efforts were often limited and met with resistance from conservative elements within the Communist Party.

Economic Crisis and Political Decline

The 1980s were marked by economic crisis and political decline, setting the stage for the eventual disintegration of Yugoslavia.

Economic Challenges

Yugoslavia faced severe economic challenges in the 1980s, including inflation, unemployment, and debt.

1. **Debt Crisis**: The country accumulated significant foreign debt due to its borrowing to finance industrialization and development projects. The debt crisis led to austerity measures and economic hardship for many citizens.
2. **Stagnation and Decline**: Economic growth stagnated, and living standards declined. The self-management system faced criticism for inefficiency and corruption, undermining public confidence in the socialist model.

Political Instability

The economic crisis exacerbated political instability, as regional and ethnic tensions intensified.

1. **Rise of Nationalism**: Nationalist leaders gained popularity by promising to address economic grievances and advocate for greater autonomy or independence. Figures like Slobodan Milošević in Serbia and Franjo Tuđman in Croatia emerged as powerful nationalist voices.

2. **Weakening of Central Authority**: The federal government struggled to maintain control, as the republics increasingly asserted their autonomy. The Communist Party's authority weakened, leading to a loss of cohesion and unity.

The Breakup of Yugoslavia

The combination of economic crisis, political instability, and rising nationalism led to the breakup of Yugoslavia in the early 1990s.

Independence Movements

Several republics declared independence, leading to a series of conflicts known as the Yugoslav Wars.

1. **Slovenia and Croatia**: Slovenia and Croatia were the first to declare independence in 1991, leading to brief but intense conflicts with the Yugoslav National Army (JNA). Both republics successfully achieved independence, but the wars marked the beginning of a violent breakup.

2. **Bosnia and Herzegovina**: The situation in Bosnia and Herzegovina was more complex, with significant populations of Serbs, Croats, and Bosniaks. The declaration of independence in 1992 led to a brutal and protracted war, characterized by ethnic cleansing and atrocities on all sides.

3. **Other Republics**: Macedonia declared independence peacefully in 1991, while Montenegro remained in a federal union with Serbia until 2006. The conflict in Kosovo in the late 1990s further complicated the breakup process.

International Involvement

The international community played a significant role in the conflicts and the eventual resolution of the Yugoslav Wars.

1. **United Nations**: The UN intervened with peacekeeping missions and diplomatic efforts to broker ceasefires and peace agreements. The UN's involvement helped mitigate some of the violence but faced criticism for its limitations.
2. **NATO**: NATO conducted military interventions, particularly in Bosnia and Herzegovina and later in Kosovo. The NATO-led intervention in Bosnia helped enforce the Dayton Agreement, which ended the Bosnian War in 1995.

Conclusion: The Legacy of the SFRY

The rise and fall of the Socialist Federal Republic of Yugoslavia had a profound impact on the region and its people.

Achievements

1. **Modernization and Development**: The SFRY achieved significant modernization and development, transforming a war-torn country into a relatively advanced and industrialized state.
2. **Non-Aligned Leadership**: Yugoslavia's leadership in the Non-Aligned Movement provided a model of independent foreign policy and contributed to global peace and cooperation efforts.
3. **Social Progress**: The government's focus on education, healthcare, and social welfare improved living standards and promoted social equality.

Challenges and Failures

1. **Ethnic Tensions**: The federal structure and centralized policies failed to fully resolve ethnic tensions, contributing to the eventual disintegration of the state.
2. **Economic Difficulties**: The economic crisis of the 1980s highlighted the limitations of the self-management system and the challenges of maintaining economic stability.
3. **Political Repression**: While achieving significant progress, the government also engaged in political repression and limited democratic freedoms.

Conclusion

The history of the Socialist Federal Republic of Yugoslavia is a complex and multifaceted story of unity and division, progress and conflict. The experiences and legacies of this unique state continue to shape the political and cultural landscape of the Balkans. As we continue our exploration of the region's history, we will examine the post-Yugoslav era, the challenges of nation-building, and the ongoing quest for peace and stability in the Balkans. The lessons learned from the rise and fall of the SFRY provide valuable insights into the challenges of managing diversity, promoting development, and achieving lasting unity in a complex and divided world.

9 798227 813497